COUNTRY LIVING
MAGAZINE

The Country Cook

100 ways to home-cooked heaven

Annie Bell

COLLINS & BROWN

First published in the United Kingdom in 2007 by
Collins & Brown Ltd
10 Southcombe Street
London
W14 0RA

An imprint of Anova Books Company Ltd

Published in association with The National
Magazine Company Limited.
Country Living is a registered trademark of
The National Magazine Company Ltd.

Project editors: Carly Madden and Barbara Dixon
Design manager: Gemma Wilson
Senior production controller: Morna McPherson

ISBN 1-84340-361-7

British Library Cataloguing-in-Publication Data:
A catalogue record for this book is available from
the British Library.

10 9 8 7 6 5 4 3 2

Reproduction by Anorax Imaging, UK
Printed and bound by Craft Print International
Ltd, Singapore

This book can be ordered direct from the
publisher.

Contact the marketing department, but try your
bookshop first.

www.anovabooks.com

Contents

Foreword

Welcome to *The Country Cook*, which gathers between hard covers the cream of Annie Bell's recipes in *Country Living* Magazine.

Annie has been writing award-winning cookery features for our food pages for four years now and her work wins new admirers with every issue. Primarily, of course, this is because her recipes are tried and tested at home and meet the practical demands of real family life, high days and holidays in our busy world. They really work.

Annie's style is warm, generous and firmly rooted in tradition, yet as modern as tomorrow, and it goes without saying that her dishes celebrate seasonal produce. For the confident cook she offers inspiration, while for the novice her clear directions and observations give the assurance that brings success.

Her words are brought to life by *Country Living* Magazine's glorious food photography. The pages look good enough to eat – you can almost smell the pie that is just out of the oven, or the sausages sizzling.

I hope you will enjoy *The Country Cook* and that you find dishes here that will become such firm favourites with your family and friends that you turn to the food pages of the magazine every month. You can also visit our website www.countryliving.co.uk to find more.

Susy Smith
Editor
Country Living Magazine

Introduction

Having waved goodbye to the last of some twenty guests who gamely camped in our garden over a long weekend, I felt that by rights I should have been feeling utterly exhausted. Instead of which I felt as though I'd had a lovely, brief holiday. It was filled with old friendships, people who had known each other for many years, and new ones. I find it magical the way that a gaggle of children, having never met before, can form instant bonds, scurrying off to the furthest corners of the garden together within minutes of being introduced. It has fused in my mind as a haze of laughter and warmth, and innocent fun. The weekend also seemed like one rolling meal – we ate and drank for England. But at no point did the cooking involved seem arduous.

Over the years, I've honed how I cook in the country, and be it weekdays, high days or holidays, somehow it always spells relaxation. This in part is through a lack of ambition; the leisured mood that settles in the countryside doesn't lend itself to tying myself in knots trying to turn out a succession of complicated dishes. I'd rather take my time and really enjoy making a main course, and then pick up a convenient cake or pastry from a local deli, or some gorgeous hunk of cheese and a bag of nuts. So on Sunday night we had steaming bowls of lentil, fennel and watercress soup, followed by a spread of pungent runny cheeses, local ham, big bowls of salad and cobnuts to crack, and then some apple tart and cream.

I frequently cheat at starters, buying in a selection of salamis to serve with pickled walnuts, gherkins and radishes, settled on a tray in front of the fire for people to pick at before we sit down. Otherwise some oysters, or a big bowl of prawns with mayonnaise, all of which are a treat but don't actually involve any cooking. And if my conscience niggles at all, then I ease it by reminding myself that I am also supporting local producers and specialised shops. At most I might rustle up something in the way of finger food, little rolls of air-dried ham wrapped around some goat's cheese, drizzled with honey and popped into a hot oven. And it takes no time to whisk up a frittata, which can be cut into slivers for handing round with a drink.

There's a certain type of food that fits the bill in the country. It's hearty, bold and full of big flavours. It might be a casserole of slowly braised beef, some chunky sausages roasted in the oven with a mustard mash, or crisp stuffed sardines hot from the grill in the summer with big bowls of colourful salads alongside. It is food that can be plonked on the table and dished out with over-sized spoons and ladles, and which possesses the yummy factor that is a sure route to contentment.

Equally, though, it might be a big earthy cauldron of soup with a ladle beside it, and a basket of crusty bread warm from the oven with a pat of chilled unsalted butter.

In fact, whenever I find myself on a long journey this is exactly what I start dreaming of: a glass of wine and a warm kitchen filled with the steaming scent of soup are a traveller's reward.

It is heartening that 'local' has become the buzz word on discerning shoppers' lips, and country cooks have a huge advantage here over city dwellers. Producers and stalls at farmers' markets will almost certainly hail from the vicinity. Specialised shops too are likely to be supporting small producers in the area. Supermarkets in this country have always, in my eyes, been a lost opportunity. They should ideally be acting as a co-operative to market the produce of small farmers nearby, as they do in many cases in Italy, France and Spain. The emphasis in this country on centralisation has sadly eroded our regional heritage. But this book is not a political rant, so enough of that.

Back to how to cook and enjoy it. Cooking in the country also has to do with good husbandry. Looking back through old cookery books spanning the centuries, I am not always sure whether I would like to travel back there. What I do envy are the systems that were necessarily built into the way people ate. In the absence of being able to pop to the supermarket for a ready meal, forward planning was an essential time-saving device. The Sunday roast, far from being the culmination of the week's cooking, was the start of it, and would stretch for several days, eaten cold with a salad, or minced in a pie or patty, and finally the bones would be used to make stock for a soup or rice.

Cooking today with tomorrow in mind was more positive and dynamic than simply using up leftovers. I love the way the weeks and seasons had a rhythm or pattern, shaped by the produce and by the days themselves. This kind of forward planning is about determinedly cooking more of an ingredient or dish than you know you will need that day or evening, because there are so many uses for it within the days to come. And wherever possible I have tried to build this into the recipes that follow, so that you're not necessarily starting from scratch. But even if you are, then hopefully it will still be a pleasure.

1

Something Small

This is one for when you have your lazy hat on; as a starter it takes little or no time to throw together. Rolls of air-dried ham with melted goat's cheese inside are great as finger food or served on a small plate with a few rocket leaves. Despite its Continental derivation, this translates beautifully to more local produce, as suggested. (For stockists see page 202.)

Grilled goat's cheese and prosciutto rolls with honey

Serves 6

125g hard goat's cheese, such as Woolsery or Ticklemore, cut into 1cm dice
1 tsp thyme leaves
2 tbsp extra virgin olive oil

12 slices air-dried ham
1 tbsp runny honey
rocket leaves, to serve

Toss the cheese and thyme with 1 tablespoon of the olive oil in a bowl. Spoon a little near the end of each slice of ham and roll up. Arrange them in a baking dish, spaced slightly apart. They can be prepared to this point in advance, in which case cover and chill.

When ready to cook, heat the oven to 210°C (190°C fan oven) gas mark 7. Drizzle the honey over the rolls, then drizzle over the remaining olive oil and bake for 7–10 minutes.

Serve either as finger food, or place the rolls on top of a few rocket leaves on little plates and drizzle the juices over.

This is a royal treatment for a humble fish, especially when made with decent kippers. In imitation, these fish are a lurid shade of what they should have been had they hung in the fireplace. It's all to do with cost-cutting – deep yellow dyes gained in popularity post-World War Two as a way of reducing the time the fish spent being smoked.

And unlike good smoked haddock, much of which comes filleted these days, good kippers will nearly always be sold on the bone. The whole fish, slit open, looks like a kite, a familiar silhouette that makes me want to take them back to where they came from in Scotland, string them up over a fire on a beach, with a loaf of brown bread and some butter on the side, and go for a long walk while they gently cook. If you do feel like a kipper feast for breakfast, then this can be prepared on the back of it.

Potted fish, as well as being salty and buttery, should have a discernible peppery kick and a subtle undertone of mace (or, failing that, a little nutmeg) to work its particular magic. The essential asides here are a pile of wafer-thin, crisp wholemeal toast and the pale heart of a romaine lettuce or some radishes.

Potted kippers

Serves 6

900g whole kippers
150ml dry white wine
black pepper
200g unsalted butter
a knife-tip of ground mace or nutmeg
cayenne pepper, to taste
3 tbsp finely chopped chives

a couple of squeezes of lemon juice,
    or 1 tsp white wine vinegar
30g (2 tbsp) small capers

To serve
thin, crisp, wholemeal toast
inner romaine leaves

Place the kippers in a large saucepan with the wine and a grinding of black pepper. Bring the liquid to the boil, then cover and cook over a low heat for 5–10 minutes until the centre of the flesh is opaque rather than translucent. Transfer the fish to a plate and simmer the juices to reduce to a couple of tablespoons. Once the fish is cool enough to handle, remove the flesh from the bones and break it up, but don't worry about the fine, hair-like bones that will be imperceptible on eating.

Melt half the butter in a large frying pan, add the fish and stir to coat. Season with mace or nutmeg and cayenne pepper to taste, then stir in the chives, lemon juice or vinegar and the reduced cooking juices. Either divide the mixture between six 150ml (9cm) ramekins, or transfer it to a large shallow dish, and press the fish down. Cover with clingfilm and chill for about an hour until it has begun to set.

Scatter the capers onto the surface, melt the remaining butter and pour this over. Cover the ramekins or dish and chill for several hours or overnight.

Serve with freshly made toast and some crisp lettuce leaves.

A big bowl of thick vegetable soup followed by a homemade pâté and salad is a treat of a lineup that will entertain a sizeable number without breaking the bank – the best kind of kitchen supper. The pâté is also useful for spreading on little croutes with a smidgeon of chutney to pass round with drinks.

A chicken liver parfait sells itself on texture – it's half butter to begin with, a cholesterol-rich treat that melts in the mouth like a poor man's foie gras pâté. To bolster the pretence, a small glass of sweet wine slips down like nectar in its company.

Accompany this with some thin, crisp toast, made with walnut or onion bread, or brioche, and a small green salad such as watercress or lamb's lettuce, simply dressed with balsamic vinegar and olive oil; alternatively a few chicory leaves. I'm partial to apple in a chicken liver parfait, but you can leave it out if you prefer.

Chicken liver and apple parfait

Serves 6

200g unsalted butter
I apple, peeled, cored and finely diced
450g chicken livers, fatty membranes removed
I bay leaf
2 sprigs of thyme
I shallot, peeled and finely chopped
I garlic clove, peeled and finely chopped
2 tbsp port

2 heaped tbsp crème fraîche
sea salt and black pepper
freshly grated nutmeg

To finish
a few bay leaves
50g–100g unsalted butter

Melt 25g of the butter for the parfait in a large frying pan over a medium heat and fry the apple, stirring frequently, for about 5 minutes until soft. Transfer this to a bowl and add another 25g of butter to the pan.

When the foam starts to subside, add the chicken livers and the herbs and sauté for 2–3 minutes, turning the livers halfway through, until they are golden on the outside but still pink in the centre. Discard the herbs and tip the chicken livers with any juices into a blender.

Add another knob of butter to the pan and sweat the shallot and garlic for a couple of minutes until glossy and translucent. Add the port and simmer until well reduced.

Tip the contents of the frying pan into the blender, add the crème fraîche, 1 teaspoon of salt and a generous grinding of black pepper, then purée. Leave this to cool in the blender for about 30 minutes.

Dice the remaining butter, add to the blender and blend until the parfait is really smooth and creamy. Season with a grinding of nutmeg and a little more salt if it needs it. Transfer the purée to a bowl and fold in the apple, then spoon the pâté into a bowl (I often use a 26cm/1 litre gratin dish) and smooth the surface.

To finish the pâté, arrange a few bay leaves in the centre. Melt 50g–100g of butter (you will need more butter to cover the surface of a shallow bowl than a deep one) in a small saucepan over a low heat, skim off the surface foam and pour the clear yellow liquid on top of the pâté, discarding the milky residue. Cover and chill overnight. It keeps well for at least 48 hours in the fridge.

When you feel like pushing the boat out for a starter or light lunch, a jellied fish terrine is a beautiful thing to behold, especially served with a spoonful of crème fraîche and slivers of smoked salmon, which provide a lovely contrast to the monkfish and prawns. But you could serve the jellied fish alone with the crème fraîche and a few salad leaves.

Jellied fish terrine

Serves 6

400ml dry white wine
sea salt and black pepper
250g monkfish (filleted weight), or other firm
    white fish, cut into 1cm dice
250g raw shelled prawns, halved across
⅔ of a sachet of gelatine
    (or sufficient leaves to set 400ml liquid*)
50g French beans (trimmed weight)

50g carrot (trimmed weight)
50g courgette (trimmed weight)
2 tsp finely chopped coriander leaves

To serve
4 heaped tbsp crème fraîche
2 tbsp finely chopped chives
225g sliced smoked salmon

Bring the wine to the boil in a small saucepan. Season the fish and poach in the wine for 2 minutes, then remove it to a bowl. Repeat with the prawns.

Sprinkle the gelatine over a couple of tablespoons of boiling water in a small bowl and leave it for a few minutes to dissolve. If it hasn't dissolved completely, stand the bowl inside a second bowl of boiling water and give it a few minutes longer, then stir again.* Combine this with the wine.

To clarify the liquid, pour it into a sieve lined with kitchen paper over a bowl, and leave it for 30 minutes to drip through. Halfway into this, add any liquid given out by the fish. At the end, cover the liquid and chill it for 3 hours until it has begun to set.

Towards the end of this time, bring a medium pan of salted water to the boil. Slice the French beans into 1cm lengths and cut the carrot and courgette into similar-sized pieces. Boil the carrot and French beans for 1 minute, add the courgette and cook for a further minute, then drain.

Fold the fish, vegetables and coriander into the jelly and transfer to a 1 litre glass serving bowl, or to small glass bowls. Combine the crème fraîche and chives. Serve the jellied fish with the crème fraîche mixture and the smoked salmon.

*If using gelatine leaves, cut them into broad strips, then place in a bowl, cover with cold water and leave to soak for 5 minutes. Drain. Pour over a little of the hot wine and stir to dissolve, then combine with the wine.

I always like to cook plenty of grilled and blanched vegetables, regardless of how much I need at the time, especially in the summer. They are great for frittatas – as the temperature rises, the call comes from those small, Italian backstreet restaurants with their pots of chilled minestrone and blackened frying pans holding cold omelettes that tempt passers-by to take a pavement seat and order a chilled glass of Pinot Grigio.

Frittatas are a winning way with eggs and bypass the usual sleight of hand called for in flipping or rolling omelettes out of the pan. They are cooked first on the hob in a frying pan and then put under the grill until they are puffy and golden. This frittata relies on grilled young courgettes, another great stand-by that can be served as an antipasto with sliced mozzarella, salami and olives, or scattered with pine nuts. Larger courgettes can be thickly sliced lengthways and grilled. Eat this thinly sliced as an appetiser, or as a light lunch or supper.

Courgette frittata

Serves 4

350g baby courgettes, ends trimmed,
    halved lengthways
4 tbsp extra virgin olive oil
sea salt and black pepper

6 medium eggs
50g freshly grated Parmesan
a large handful of basil leaves, torn in half
25g finely sliced Parmesan

Heat a ridged griddle over a medium heat. Place the courgettes in a large bowl, drizzle over 2 tablespoons of the olive oil, add some seasoning and toss to coat them. Cook the courgettes in one or two batches. Lay them out in the pan in a single layer, turn them as they colour on the underside and cook the second side. Transfer to a plate – they don't have to be completely cool before the next stage, but can be cooked in advance if you wish.

Whisk the eggs in a bowl, then stir in the grated Parmesan, basil and some seasoning. Fold in the grilled courgettes.

Heat an overhead grill to high and also heat a 26cm frying pan with a heatproof handle over a medium heat. Add 1 tbsp of the oil to the pan, tip in the egg and courgette mixture and cook for 3 minutes. Scatter the Parmesan slices over the top of the omelette, drizzle over the remaining oil and place under the grill for 3–4 minutes until golden and puffy at the sides. The omelette can be eaten hot or at room temperature.

Roulades are part of the extended family of soufflés, one that is held in awe and trepidation by many, but no-one should fear a roulade, given that there's not a lot to sink. This one comprises a thin, moussey blanket lined with paper-thin slices of salty, air-dried ham, and cream cheese within.

There is something particularly alluring about the snailshell spiral of a roulade, confirmed by our fondness for Swiss rolls. As well as making a very elegant first course, when it will stretch to serve eight with a few salad leaves, this will also stand as a main course if the mood is light, in which case it's good for four to six bods.

Mushroom and bresaola roulade

Serves 4–6

For the roulade
75g unsalted butter, plus extra for greasing
600g flat-cap mushrooms, stalks trimmed if
   necessary
sea salt and black pepper
5 medium eggs
75g plain flour, sifted

For the filling
250g mascarpone
70g finely sliced bresaola
a few handfuls of young spinach leaves
coarsely chopped flat-leaf parsley, to serve

To make the roulade, heat the oven to 200°C (180°C fan oven) gas mark 6. Butter a 23cm x 33cm Swiss roll tin, line it with baking paper and butter this also. Finely chop the mushrooms in batches in a food processor, almost to a purée, or, failing this, with a large, sharp knife.

If you are clever about the next stage, and place the bowl with the eggs next to the stove, you should be able to whisk them at the same time as frying the mushrooms. Melt the butter in a large frying pan over a medium heat, add the mushrooms and some seasoning and fry for 20–25 minutes, stirring occasionally, until the purée dries out and starts to separate into clumps. Break the eggs into a large bowl and, using an electric whisk, whisk for about 8 minutes until almost white and mousse-like. You can also do this in a food processor using the whisking attachment, in which case reduce the time to about 5 minutes.

Lightly fold in the flour in two goes, then the mushrooms. Pour the mixture into the prepared tin and smooth it using the back of a spoon. Don't worry about it rising a little above the top of the tin – it will level as it cooks. Bake for 10 minutes until lightly golden and springy to the touch.

Lay out a clean tea towel. Run a knife around the edge of the roulade and turn it out onto the towel. Roll it up with the tea towel, leaving the paper in place and starting at the short end so you end up with a short, fat roll. Leave to cool for 40–60 minutes.

To fill the roulade, unroll it and remove the paper. Using a palette knife, spread the mascarpone over the surface, then cover this with a layer of bresaola, and then a layer of spinach leaves. Using the tea towel, roll the sponge up again and tip it onto a serving plate, seam downwards. Scatter over a little chopped parsley. If not serving it at once, cover and chill, then bring it back up to room temperature 30 minutes before eating.

These soufflés look and taste divine, and for the cook they are the answer to all the usual problems posed by timing, since they are made in advance and popped back into the oven for 15 minutes before eating. And, like most soufflés, they're a star at pretty much any occasion – just build everything else around them.

There are excellent goat's cheeses made by small producers (see page 202). Otherwise I would go for a chèvre log, which has just the right balance of flavour and texture.

Twice-baked goat's cheese and thyme soufflés

Serves 6

300ml full-cream milk

½ onion, peeled and sliced

6 cloves

50g unsalted butter, plus extra for greasing

45g plain flour

1 x 150g mature goat's cheese, rind discarded,
  grated

sea salt and black pepper

3 medium eggs, separated

300ml double cream

1 tbsp thyme leaves

3 tbsp freshly grated Parmesan

Heat the oven to 200°C (180°C fan oven) gas mark 6. Put the milk with the onion and cloves in a small saucepan and bring to the boil, then take off the heat and leave to infuse for 15 minutes. Melt the butter in a small, non-stick saucepan over a medium heat, stir in the flour and cook the roux for a minute or two until floury in appearance. Now strain the milk and, working off the heat, gradually beat it into the roux using a wooden spoon. Return the mixture to a medium heat and cook for several minutes, stirring until it is really thick and glossy.

Remove from the heat, stir in the goat's cheese and season with salt and pepper. Let it cool for a few minutes while you whisk the egg whites in a bowl until stiff. Fold the egg yolks into the cheese sauce, and then the egg whites in three goes.

Butter six 150ml (9cm) ramekins and divide the mixture between them. Place these in a 30cm x 20cm roasting dish, with boiling water to come halfway up the sides of the ramekins and bake for 15 minutes until the soufflés are risen and lightly coloured. Remove and leave them to cool in the roasting tin, where they will sink. Run a knife around the edge of the soufflés and gently prise them out, then arrange them back in the roasting dish, having drained and dried it. The soufflés can be prepared to this point in advance, up to the night before, in which case cover the dish and chill them.

To serve, heat the oven to 220°C (200°C fan oven) gas mark 7. Season the cream and pour over the soufflés, then scatter over the thyme and Parmesan. Bake for another 15 minutes until they are risen and crusty on the surface. Serve immediately.

PASTRY

Pastry thrives on a light touch, which is why food processors do such a great job. There is no chance for the butter to soften with warmth in the brief whizz of the blade. Otherwise, think cool – chilled butter, cold fingers and a marble slab for rolling it out supply the perfect conditions.

Making a tart case

225g plain flour, plus extra for dusting
a pinch of sea salt

150g unsalted butter, chilled and diced
1 medium egg, separated

Place the flour and salt in the bowl of a food processor, add the butter and whizz to a fine, crumb-like consistency.

Incorporate the egg yolk, then with the motor running trickle in just enough cold water for the dough to cling together in lumps.

Transfer the pastry to a large bowl and, using your hands, bring it together into a ball. (You can, of course, do all of this by hand, rubbing in the butter with your fingers.)

Wrap the pastry in clingfilm and chill for at least 1 hour, though it will keep in the fridge for up to two days. It also freezes well, so you may like to make a second batch while you are at it.

Baking the tart case blind

Heat the oven to 190°C (170°C fan oven) gas mark 5. Knead the pastry until it is pliable, and roll it out thinly on a lightly floured surface.

Carefully lift it into a 23cm x 6cm tart tin with a removable base – it's quite a durable pastry and shouldn't tear or collapse. Press it into the corners of the tin and trim the top using a knife. Reserve the trimmings to patch the pastry case if necessary after it has been baked.

Prick the base with a fork and line it with a sheet of foil, tucking it over the top to secure the pastry sides to the tin. Now weight it with baking beans – a packet of pulses such as dried chickpeas will do nicely.

Bake the case for 15 minutes, then remove the foil and baking beans. If any of the sides have shrunk more than they should, use a little of the reserved pastry to patch them. Remember the case can only be filled as far as the lowest point of the sides.

Brush the base and sides of the case with the reserved egg white, then bake it for another 10 minutes until lightly coloured. This glaze helps to seal the pastry and prevent the filling from soaking into it.

Good quiches have everything to do with an unctuously creamy filling, that lovely loose set that hovers between holding together and falling apart. Few vegetables shine more brightly than onions, which, when slowly sweated, can melt the heart of anything they are added to.

Anything this good can pass muster served as a sliver, as well as a more generous slice, with a pile of thickly sliced air-dried ham in the environ.

Onion tart

Serves 6

23cm x 6cm tart case, baked blind
  (see pages 26–27)

For the filling
40g unsalted butter
6 Spanish onions (about 1.4kg), peeled, halved
  and thinly sliced

sea salt and black pepper
300g crème fraîche
2 medium eggs
I tbsp soft thyme leaves
150g freshly grated Parmesan

Melt the butter in a large saucepan over a low heat, add the onions, scatter over 1 teaspoon of salt and sweat for at least 40 minutes until creamy and soft, without allowing them to colour. Stir more frequently towards the end, when they may stick a little, and turn the heat down if necessary. This period of cooking is all-important to both the flavour and texture of the onions – it takes time to render them subtly sweet and silky.

Heat the oven to 190°C (170°C fan oven) gas mark 5. In a large bowl, whisk the crème fraîche with the eggs, some pepper, a little more of the salt, the thyme and half the Parmesan. Stir in the cooked onions and pour the mixture into the prepared tart case. Scatter over the remaining Parmesan and bake for 30–35 minutes until golden on the surface and set.

Leave the tart to stand for 20 minutes before serving. This is almost nicer eaten at room temperature, when it is supremely creamy.

These are lovely in-hand food to graze on wherever, either with a few lightly dressed salad leaves on top as a starter, or cut into quarters to pass around as a nibble with drinks. They are also sufficiently pizza-like to appeal to most children, in which case I find you need twice the number.

Tomato tarts

Serves 6

350g puff pastry
flour for dusting
Dijon mustard
10–12 small tomatoes on the vine, thinly sliced

1 medium egg yolk blended with 1 tbsp water
sea salt and black pepper
30g finely shaved Parmesan
extra virgin olive oil

Heat the oven to 220°C (200°C fan oven) gas mark 7.

Thinly roll out the pastry on a lightly floured worksurface – I roll out half at a time – and, using a bowl or a plate as a guide, cut out six 12cm circles. Arrange these on a couple of baking trays.

Spread a little Dijon mustard in the centre of each pastry circle, to within about 1cm of the rim. Arrange the tomato slices on top in an overlapping circle, with one of the end slices positioned in the centre. You can reserve any leftovers for making a soup or sauce. Brush the surrounding rim with the eggwash, then season the tomatoes, top with a few slivers of Parmesan, drizzle over a little olive oil and bake in the oven for 15–20 minutes until golden and risen. Serve hot or cold.

While macaroni in cheese sauce is a loved and hallowed classic, there is a lengthy list of contenders when it comes to pasta shape – I use garganelli, a delicate egg pasta that looks like a scroll, and penne is a good all-rounder. The mushrooms should be nice and meaty – shiitake stand out among cultivated ones, while porcini and girolles would both be divine. Ah yes, and you could add a few drops of truffle oil should you have some. A big bowl of floppy green lettuce leaves would be lovely served with the gratin, too.

You can also prepare the gratin in advance, in which case the sauce, mushrooms and pasta should all be at room temperature before you assemble it. Having drained the pasta, toss it with a little oil to prevent it from sticking. And, because it starts at a lower temperature, bake the gratin for an additional 5 minutes.

Pasta gratin with wild mushrooms and bacon

Serves 4–6

For the gratin
200g dried egg pasta, such as penne
20g unsalted butter
1 tbsp extra virgin olive oil
250g meaty mushrooms, trimmed,
    such as shiitake
150g sliced Raclette or Fontina
6 rindless streaky bacon rashers

For the sauce
50g unsalted butter
45g plain flour
850ml full-cream milk
1 bay leaf
1 tbsp Dijon mustard
150g crème fraîche
sea salt and black pepper
freshly grated nutmeg

Heat the oven to 210°C (190°C fan oven) gas mark 7. Bring a large pan of salted water to the boil, add the pasta, give it a stir and cook until almost tender, leaving it slightly undercooked. Drain it into a sieve, quite thoroughly, then return it to the pan.

At the same time, make the sauce. Melt the butter in a non-stick saucepan over a medium heat, then stir in the flour and leave the roux to seethe for about a minute until it looks pale. Working off the heat, gradually beat in the milk – you should end up with a lump-free sauce the consistency of thin cream. Return the pan to the heat and bring to the boil, stirring constantly. Add the bay leaf and cook over a low heat for 5 minutes, then whisk in the mustard and crème fraîche. Season with salt, pepper and nutmeg.

Heat the butter for the gratin with the olive oil in a large frying pan over a medium-high heat. If using shiitake mushrooms I would leave them whole, but others might need slicing. Add the mushrooms to the pan, season with salt and pepper and sauté for several minutes until soft and starting to colour. If they give out any liquid, cook until this evaporates.

Toss the pasta with the hot sauce and mushrooms, leaving the bay leaf in or taking it out as preferred. Tip this into a 2.5 litre (35cm) gratin or other shallow ovenproof dish and mix in the sliced cheese. Lay the bacon on top and cook in the oven for 15 minutes, then give it a few minutes under the grill until golden.

Pasta, like every other food of mass consumption, has been corrupted by commercial considerations and processes. The difference between the bad and the good is that of sliced white bread and a hand-crafted loaf of sourdough, which have little in common aside from their name. Small artisanal pastifici not only fuss about the grains that go to make their semola – the variety, how they are grown, harvested and milled – but the 'trafile di bronzo' or bronze dies used in shaping the pasta.

One particular brand to look out for is Cipriani (as in the hotel in Venice). The packaging says it all: an elegant box filled with exquisitely fine brittle pasta wrapped in waxed paper.

The Ligurians say that this dish should be made with spaghetti; I think tagliardi works even better. Potatoes with pasta may seem an overstatement, but it works a treat, the potatoes absorbing the basil-scented oil of the pesto.

Tagliardi with pesto, potatoes and green beans

Serves 4

For the pesto
30g pine nuts
1 garlic clove, peeled
10 tbsp extra virgin olive oil,
    plus a little extra
sea salt and black pepper
90g basil leaves
150g freshly grated Parmesan

For the pasta
500g small waxy potatoes, peeled
150g Cipriani tagliardi
250g French beans, topped and tailed
4 handfuls of rocket leaves
a squeeze of lemon juice

To make the pesto, place the pine nuts, garlic, the 10 tbsp olive oil and some salt and pepper in the bowl of a food processor and reduce to a paste. Feed the basil leaves through the funnel with the motor running and purée. Transfer to a bowl and stir in the Parmesan. If not using straight away, cover the surface with a film of olive oil to prevent it discolouring and store in the fridge.

Bring three pans of salted water to the boil: one large for the pasta and two medium ones for the potatoes and beans. Add the potatoes to one of the medium pans, bring back to the boil and cook for 15–20 minutes until tender. Add the tagliardi to the large pan of water, which should be at a rolling boil, and cook for 4 minutes, or until tender.

At about the same time, add the beans to the third pan of water, bring back to the boil and cook for 3–5 minutes until just tender. Drain the potatoes into a sieve, tip onto a board and slice thickly. Also drain the beans. Reserving a cup of the pasta cooking water, drain the pasta into a colander and return it to the saucepan. Add the potatoes and beans to the pan, spoon over the pesto and toss. Add a good splash or two of the reserved cooking water, return the pan to the heat and cook for a couple of minutes, turning until the sauce is creamy and sizzling.

Toss the rocket leaves in a bowl with a little olive oil, a squeeze of lemon juice and a pinch of salt. Pile the pasta onto four warm plates, top with the rocket and serve.

2
Soups

Thick, warming and full of goodness, a hearty tomato soup is an essential part of anyone's culinary repertoire. Dress it up or down as suits, with slices of baguette for children to dip, or with a little seafood on the side, croutons spread with Gentleman's Relish, or leafy chopped herbs.

Tomato and chilli soup

Serves 4–6

1.5kg tomatoes

extra virgin olive oil

2 onions, peeled and chopped

2 sticks of celery, trimmed and sliced

1 heaped tsp finely chopped medium-hot chilli

4 garlic cloves, peeled and finely chopped

1 tsp balsamic vinegar

a pinch of saffron filaments (about 20)

1 tsp caster sugar

sea salt

croutons, to serve (optional)

Bring a medium pan of water to the boil. Cut out a small cone from the top of each tomato and discard. Plunge the tomatoes into the boiling water for about 20 seconds (you may need to do this in batches), and then into cold water. Slip off the skins and coarsely chop the flesh.

Heat 2 tbsp of olive oil in a large saucepan over a medium heat and sweat the onions, celery and chilli for 10–15 minutes, stirring frequently, until lightly coloured, adding the garlic halfway through. Add the balsamic vinegar and cook until it evaporates, then add the tomatoes, saffron, sugar and some salt to taste. Give them a stir, then cover and cook over a low heat for 30 minutes, stirring occasionally.

Liquidise the soup in a blender in batches, return it to a clean saucepan and taste for seasoning. Reheat and serve in warm bowls drizzled with a little olive oil, and topped with croutons, if wished.

This is a play on that classic soup vichyssoise, but is just a little bit gutsier, as befits country appetites. Don't let those leathery outer lettuce leaves go to waste – even though they reduce to water, they have a lovely milky savour and are full of goodness.

Lettuce and parsley vichyssoise

Serves 6

500g waxy potatoes, peeled or scrubbed as
    necessary, and halved or quartered if large
50g unsalted butter
280g white and pale green part of leek, sliced
3 sticks of celery heart, trimmed and sliced
outer leaves of 2 lettuces, sliced
150ml dry white wine
850ml chicken stock
sea salt and black or white pepper

2 large handfuls of flat-leaf parsley leaves
300ml single cream (1 x 284ml pot)

To serve
crisp croutons
spring onions, trimmed and sliced, or snipped
    chives
salmon roe

Bring a medium pan of salted water to the boil and cook the potatoes until tender. Drain and leave for a few minutes for the surface moisture to evaporate, then press them through a sieve.

Melt the butter in a large saucepan and sweat the leek and celery over a very low heat for about 12 minutes, stirring frequently to prevent them colouring, then add the lettuce, turn the heat up and continue to fry until it is wilted.

Add the wine and reduce until syrupy. Then add the chicken stock and some seasoning and bring to the boil. Cover the pan, turn down the heat and simmer over a low heat for 7–8 minutes.

Liquidise the soup with the parsley, return to the saucepan and whisk in the puréed potato. Stir in the cream.

Served hot: Reheat the soup without boiling and ladle into warm bowls. Serve with crisp croutons and sliced spring onions or chives.
Served cold: Serve the soup lightly chilled. Ladle it into bowls, scatter over some sliced spring onions or chives and a little salmon roe.

I have a Russian friend who starts longing for the comfort of her mother's cooking when she sees this soup simmering on the hob, whereas I am simply sold on the drama of the vermilion broth with all its treasures.

Beetroot, cabbage and apple soup

Serves 6

30g unsalted butter
150g rindless streaky bacon rashers, diced
1 onion, peeled and finely chopped
2 garlic cloves, peeled and finely chopped
¼ red cabbage, finely sliced
600g uncooked beetroot, trimmed,
    peeled and cut into 1cm dice
2 apples, peeled, cored and cut into
    1cm dice

200ml dry cider
1.2 litres chicken stock
sea salt and black pepper

To serve
crème fraîche
spring onions, trimmed and sliced

Melt the butter in a large saucepan over a medium heat and fry the bacon for about 5 minutes until lightly golden, stirring occasionally. Add the onion and garlic and fry for a few minutes longer until they start to colour, again stirring occasionally.

Halve the cabbage strips into two shorter lengths, add to the pan with the beetroot and apples, and sweat for another 5 minutes, stirring now and again.

Add the cider, turn the heat up and reduce until syrupy, then add the chicken stock and some seasoning. Bring to the boil, cover the pan and simmer over a low heat for 30–45 minutes until the beetroot is tender.

Serve with a spoonful of crème fraîche and some spring onions scattered over.

I'm not sure if this is closer to a minestrone or to a pistou, given that it has a vibrant parsley purée stirred in. Either way, it's very comforting – lots of lovely wintery veg cooked to a melting softness.

Winter minestrone soup

Serves 4

9 tbsp extra virgin olive oil
300g each swede, celeriac and carrot,
 trimmed and cut into 1cm dice
2 leeks, trimmed, quartered and sliced
2 red onions, peeled and diced
1 celery heart, trimmed and sliced
sea salt and black pepper
700ml chicken or vegetable stock

100ml dry white wine
freshly grated Parmesan, to serve (optional)

For the parsley pesto
15g pine nuts or roasted cashews
50g flat-leaf parsley leaves
1 large garlic clove, peeled and chopped

Heat 2 tablespoons of the olive oil in a large saucepan over a medium heat, add half the vegetables and fry, stirring occasionally, for 5–7 minutes until just starting to colour. Remove them to a bowl, leaving the oil behind, add another 2 tablespoons of the oil and fry the remaining vegetables in the same way. Return all the vegetables to the pan, season them well, then add the stock and wine and bring to the boil. Cover the pan, lower the heat and simmer for about 12 minutes until tender, then taste for seasoning.

To make the parsley pesto, whizz all the ingredients with the remaining oil to a purée in a food processor (if using pine nuts, first toast them in a frying pan over a medium heat, stirring, until golden).

Stir the pesto into the soup just before serving, but avoid reheating, or you will lose the green vibrancy of the parsley. Accompany with Parmesan, if wished.

Sometimes I make this using leafy chard greens, something that I am delighted is becoming increasingly easy to find, particularly in farmers' markets. It has the elegance of spinach, but with the robust nature of cabbage, and the stalks make a deliciously rich gratin: slice and blanch them, mix through with some crème fraîche and Dijon mustard, and layer with a gooey Alpine cheese. Scatter over some breadcrumbs tossed with butter and pop into a hot oven until heated through and golden.

Lentil, fennel and watercress soup

Serves 6

extra virgin olive oil
1 onion, peeled and chopped
2 fennel bulbs, trimmed and diced
3 sticks of celery, trimmed, halved lengthways
   and finely sliced
2 garlic cloves, peeled and finely chopped

250g Le Puy or French green lentils
1.7 litres chicken or vegetable stock
a pinch of dried chilli flakes
sea salt
100g watercress, coarsely chopped

Heat 3 tablespoons of olive oil in a large saucepan over a medium heat, add the onion, fennel and celery and sweat for 15–20 minutes until glossy and starting to colour, stirring occasionally and adding the garlic a couple of minutes before the end.

Add the lentils and give them a stir to coat them in the oil, then add the stock and the chilli. Bring to the boil, then simmer over a low heat for about 25 minutes, or until the lentils are just tender.

Season to taste with salt, stir in the chopped watercress and simmer for a moment longer (or a few minutes if using Swiss chard) to ensure the greens keep their brilliant colour.

Serve in warm bowls with a splash of extra virgin olive oil for those who like it.

This is a great soup to make at Christmas time, when you've cooked up a large batch of roasted veg and have plenty of leftovers. And it relies on wintery roots, which are bound to be filling any organic boxes at this time of year. A chunky soup-cum-stew is endlessly useful, and I pop all manner of tasty odds and ends into the pot. You may well have a vat of turkey or ham stock waiting in the wings, too.

Peppered sherry has a wide variety of uses – for example, to titivate a soup, stew or casserole, and to enliven a rarebit mixture or a steak and kidney pie.

Roasted vegetable, chestnut and barley soup

Serves 6

100g pearl barley
1 x recipe for Roasted roots (see page 156)
1 tbsp extra virgin olive oil
100g smoked or unsmoked rindless streaky
   bacon rashers, diced
150g cooked and peeled chestnuts, sliced

1 sprig of rosemary
sea salt and black pepper
1 litre chicken or vegetable stock
5 tbsp chopped flat-leaf parsley
peppered sherry, to serve (see below)

Bring a medium pan of water to the boil, add the pearl barley and simmer for about 1 hour until tender, then drain it.

Discard the bay leaves and thyme from the roasted roots and dice the vegetables. Squeeze out the insides of the garlic cloves, too.

Heat the olive oil in a large saucepan over a medium heat and fry the bacon for 7–8 minutes until crisp and golden, stirring occasionally. Now, add the chestnuts and rosemary needles and fry until the chestnuts begin to colour. Stir in the vegetables and garlic, season and cook for a few minutes longer.

Pour in the stock and barley and bring to the boil, then simmer for a few minutes. Add the parsley and serve sprinkled with peppered sherry. If you cook the soup ahead, you may need to add more stock before serving, as it will continue to thicken.

Peppered sherry

a few small dried chillies
500–750ml dry sherry

Put the chillies in a jar or bottle. Pour in the sherry, then seal and leave for a few days. It will become stronger with time, so taste before using.

There is a certain irony that some of today's most fashionable dishes, which make use of slightly stale bread – a measure of thrift in days gone by – now involve something of an investment before you can contemplate any of them. Our hearts' desire is that well-crafted, artisanal loaf that succeeds in being moist but chewy at the same time, with a crust that invites your teeth to grip and tear it apart. And, if we're allowed everything on our wish list, it should have been baked in a wood-fired oven, its base cast with a pale greeny-grey bloom of ashes, which all adds to the flavour.

This is one of those half-stew half-soup dishes that rely on such bread, and which seem to define Mediterranean comfort food. The first time I ate this at Moro I dreamt of it all night long, so it was a joy to come across the recipe in Sam and Sam Clark's cookbook *Casa Moro*. Bread and caraway seeds are what give the soup its distinctive texture and flavour. Try to cook your own beans – they are a world apart from tinned in this recipe, and you will have the stock to fall back on, too.

Turkish village soup with bread and caraway

Serves 4

8 tbsp extra virgin olive oil, plus extra to serve

1 large onion, peeled and finely chopped

3 large carrots, trimmed, peeled and finely chopped

4 sticks of celery, trimmed and finely chopped

sea salt and black pepper

4 garlic cloves, peeled and thinly sliced

3 tsp caraway seeds

3 tbsp roughly chopped flat-leaf parsley

1 x 400g tin whole plum tomatoes, drained of juice and broken up

500g white cabbage, thinly sliced and chopped

1.25 litres water, or 1 litre and 250ml bean liquor

400g cooked borlotti or pinto beans (200g dried weight), or 2 x 400g tins, drained and rinsed

200g day-old ciabatta or rustic white sourdough bread, crusts removed and torn into bite-sized pieces

Heat the olive oil in a large saucepan over a medium heat, add the onion, carrots, celery and a pinch of salt and fry gently for 15–20 minutes, stirring occasionally, until the vegetables begin to turn golden.

Add the garlic, caraway and half the parsley and fry for 1–2 minutes, then add the tomatoes. Cook for another 5–8 minutes, again stirring occasionally. Add the cabbage and water or stock and bring to the boil, then simmer over a low heat for 20 minutes until the cabbage is almost cooked.

Add the beans and simmer for a further 10 minutes, stirring frequently until the cabbage is tender.

Remove from the heat and taste for seasoning, then stir in the bread and the rest of the parsley. Leave for 5 minutes for the bread to absorb the liquid. The soup should be thick, almost like a stew; if it is too dry, add a little more water or bean liquor. Serve drizzled with extra virgin olive oil.

There is no match for suet in a dumpling; it renders them supremely light and fluffy – these sinful, pudgy little cushions are moistened by broth and showered with grated Parmesan. It's in the same mindset as settling down to a mound of mashed potato with a pat of salty butter and nothing else in attendance. It doesn't get much more soothing, so light the fire and warm your slippers.

Bacon and sage dumplings in broth

Serves 4

For the dumplings
100g rindless streaky bacon rashers, coarsely
    sliced
120g fresh white breadcrumbs (see page 62)
100g shredded suet
about 8 sage leaves, finely chopped
3 medium egg yolks
sea salt and black pepper

For the soup
800ml chicken stock
100ml dry white wine

To serve
coarsely chopped flat-leaf parsley
freshly grated Parmesan

Place the bacon in the bowl of a food processor and finely chop it. Add the breadcrumbs, suet, sage, egg yolks and some seasoning and whizz until the mixture looks sticky, then add just enough water for the dough to start to cling together in lumps. Shape the dough into balls the size of a cherry and place on a plate. Cover and chill if not cooking them very soon.

To cook the dumplings, bring the stock and wine to the boil with a little salt in a large saucepan, then lower the heat and simmer for 15 minutes. Add the dumplings and poach, over a low heat, for another 10 minutes.

Ladle into bowls and serve scattered with parsley and lots of freshly grated Parmesan.

This is an Anglo-Indian take on a curried soup, with the suspicion of a few spices to lend it some charm. I suppose that shelling mussels belongs in the same time-consuming category as stuffing mushrooms, but it's a small luxury and small luxuries bring pleasure, so I never resent the ten or so minutes it takes.

Curried mussel soup with saffron

Serves 4

1.5kg mussels
100ml dry white wine
25g unsalted butter
4 leeks, trimmed and sliced
1 onion, peeled and finely chopped
1 garlic clove, peeled and finely chopped
½–1 tsp curry powder (depending on heat)
a pinch of saffron filaments (about 20), infused in
    1 tbsp boiling water for 15 minutes

1 tbsp Cognac
150ml fish or chicken stock
100g crème fraîche
1 tsp plain flour, blended with 1 tsp unsalted
    butter
chopped coriander leaves, to serve

Wash the mussels in a sink of cold water, pulling off the beards and discarding any that are broken or do not close when tapped sharply. Give them a second rinse, then place them in a large saucepan with the wine. Cover the pan and cook over a high heat for about 5 minutes, shaking the pan once, until they open.

Tip the mussels into a colander set over a bowl to collect the juices and discard any that have not opened. When they are cool enough to handle, shell two-thirds of them. Reserve the shelled and unshelled mussels in a bowl. You can prepare them to this point up to a couple of hours in advance, in which case cover and chill them.

Melt the butter in a large saucepan over a medium heat, add the leeks and onion and fry for about 8 minutes until glossy, stirring occasionally, and adding the garlic just before the end. Stir in the curry powder, then the saffron infusion, Cognac, stock and mussel liquor, discarding the gritty bit at the bottom of the bowl. Bring this to the boil, then cover the pan and simmer for 10 minutes. Stir in the crème fraîche and the flour and butter paste, and stir until this melts.

Finally, add the mussels and cook gently for a few minutes just to heat them through. Be careful not to overcook them or they will toughen. Serve in warmed bowls, scattered with coriander.

Mussels and potatoes work uncommonly well together, their differing textures offsetting each other's charms to a 'T'. A chowder also makes full use of all those lovely salty juices, enhanced by lots of cream – it would take more than a little effort to achieve the same intensity with stock in another soup. A good fishmonger will have his eye on the size and flavour of the mussels, though the former is no indicator of quality – diminutive dark orange mussels are frequently the tastiest.

Mussel chowder

Serves 4

2kg mussels
40g unsalted butter
3 leeks, trimmed and sliced
sea salt and black pepper
200ml crème fraîche
200ml full-cream milk

a pinch of saffron filaments (about 20), infused
    in 1 tbsp boiling water for 15 minutes
400g cooked maincrop or waxy potatoes,
    cut into 1cm dice
coarsely chopped flat-leaf parsley

Wash the mussels in a sink of cold water, pulling off the beards and discarding any that are broken or do not close when tapped sharply. Give them a second rinse, then place them in a large saucepan, cover the pan and cook over a high heat for about 5 minutes, shaking the pan once, until they open.

Tip the mussels into a colander set over a bowl to collect the juices and discard any that have not opened. When they are cool enough to handle, shell three-quarters of them and reserve together with the unshelled mussels.

Melt the butter in a large frying pan over a medium heat. Season the leeks and sauté them for 7–10 minutes until they are lightly coloured and soft.

Pour the mussel liquor into a medium saucepan, discarding the last little gritty bit. Add the crème fraîche, milk, saffron infusion and some black pepper and bring to a simmer. Add the leeks, potatoes and mussels and heat through, then taste for seasoning.

Serve the chowder in bowls scattered with parsley.

3

Meat

Nada Saleh is a superb Middle Eastern cook, and come the summer I often riffle through her collections of spicy salads and finger foods for barbecues. This comes from her book *Fresh Moroccan*.

Lamb koftas

Makes 12 x 20cm skewers

500g minced lamb
25g coriander leaves, finely chopped
25g flat-leaf parsley leaves, finely chopped
1 small onion, peeled and finely chopped

¼ tsp cayenne pepper
1 tsp ground cumin
1 tsp sea salt

If using wooden skewers, soak them in cold water for a few minutes.

Combine all the ingredients in a bowl. Shape the koftas as two small sausages on each skewer: take pieces of the mixture, the size of a walnut, and mould them around each end of a skewer by closing your hand around it and squeezing. You should end up with about 12 skewers.

Outdoors: Barbecue for 10–15 minutes in total, turning them as necessary.
Indoors: Place a ridged griddle over a medium-hot heat and cook the koftas for 7–10 minutes.

I use the term 'fresh' with breadcrumbs only to distinguish them from the dried orange ones that come in packets. They still need to be made with bread that is a couple of days old. A well-crafted loaf starts to dry out after a few days (stale is something of an unkind description, suggesting it is no longer appetising to eat), when its newfound dryness is what affords it another lease of life. The closest in convenience is a loaf of ciabatta, which is dry to begin with. But otherwise hunting grounds are small delis where the bread is baked traditionally, a stall at a farmers' market, or of course you could make your own. Simply remove the crusts, tear the crumb into pieces and whizz it in a food processor. Breadcrumbs also freeze well.

Casserole of lamb shanks with dumplings

Serves 4

For the casserole
1 tbsp olive or vegetable oil
sea salt and black pepper
3–4 lamb shanks (leg or shoulder)
300ml dry white wine
300ml water
1 bay leaf
3 sprigs of thyme
1 head of garlic, cloves peeled
about 30 saffron filaments, infused in 1 tbsp
    boiling water for 15 minutes
3 large carrots, trimmed, peeled and thickly
    sliced diagonally

4 sticks of celery, trimmed and thickly sliced
3 good-sized turnips, trimmed, peeled, halved
    and thickly sliced
coarsely chopped flat-leaf parsley, to serve

For the dumplings
120g fresh breadcrumbs
120g shredded suet
3 medium egg yolks
1 heaped tbsp grainy mustard
2–3 tbsp milk or water

Heat the oil in a large cast-iron or other heavy casserole over a medium heat, season the lamb shanks and sear to colour them all over. Add the wine, water, herbs, garlic and saffron infusion and bring to the boil, then cover the pan and simmer for 1 hour 40 minutes, turning the shanks after 1 hour. Add the vegetables and cook for a further 20 minutes – they should be just tender. Taste the juices for seasoning.

The dumplings can be made in advance of the casserole, or while it is cooking. Place the breadcrumbs, suet, egg yolks, mustard and some seasoning in a food processor and whizz until the mixture looks sticky, then add just enough milk or water for the dough to start to cling together in lumps. Shape the dough into balls a little smaller than a walnut and place on a plate. Cover and chill them if not cooking soon.

To cook the dumplings, bring a large pan of water to the boil, add them and poach over a low heat for 10 minutes. Remove them with a slotted spoon and serve with the lamb, vegetables and juices, scattered with the chopped parsley.

A loin is to lamb what fillet steak is to beef, and here it is stuffed with slivers of dried apricot and pistachios. It comes very close to a charming recipe by Margaret Costa in her *Four Seasons Cookery Book* for a stuffed shoulder, a favourite when I first began cooking, which against the odds I managed to produce in a Baby Belling in our tiny garret flat, if that's some recommendation of how simple it is.

But there are loins and loins. The smallest weigh in at about a pound, are free from fat and meltingly tender, while larger ones from hogget or shearling – lamb that is over a year old – can be double that size. And these are the choice cuts – you have the treat of sweet, loose-grained flesh, basted by the copious fat that surrounds it, a real gourmand's treat.

This is so deliciously delicate and succulent, I would opt for little more than a dish of purple sprouting broccoli laced with slivers of salty butter, and another of new potatoes with even more salty butter and sprigs of mint, gathered at the last minute.

A couple of loins this size will do nicely for six, but if you are four then a single, slightly larger one, about 700–800g, will do.

Roast loin of lamb with apricot and pistachio stuffing

Serves 6

120g unsalted butter
1 onion, peeled and finely chopped
130g ready-to-eat dried apricots, thinly sliced
70g shelled raw pistachios, finely chopped
finely grated zest of 1 lemon

sea salt and black pepper
70ml dry white wine
2 x 600g boned and rolled loins of lamb
vegetable oil

You can stuff the loins in advance. Melt the butter in a large frying pan over a medium heat, add the onion and fry for several minutes, stirring occasionally, until softened and lightly coloured. Add the apricots, pistachios, lemon zest and some seasoning and fry for 2 minutes longer, stirring occasionally. Add the wine and cook until absorbed, then continue to cook for a couple more minutes until nicely softened. Transfer the stuffing to a bowl and leave to cool.

Untie and unroll the loins. Open them out and cut through to the skin down the centre to make room for the stuffing. Divide the stuffing between them, spreading it down the middle, then reroll and tie them. Cover and chill if not cooking immediately.

When ready to cook, heat the oven to 210°C (190°C fan oven) gas mark 7. Place a medium frying pan with a heatproof handle, or a roasting dish, over a medium-high heat. Pour a little oil into the palm of your hand, rub your hands together and lightly coat the lamb, then season it and sear to colour (don't worry about the ends). Roast (calculating 25 minutes for the first 500g, and 17 minutes per 500g thereafter).

Transfer the lamb to a warm plate to rest for 10 minutes. Slice and serve with the gravy.

A jug of rich brown gravy

2 tbsp groundnut or vegetable oil
500g mixture of diced onion, celery, leek and
  carrot
2 garlic cloves, peeled and finely chopped

2 tsp plain flour
150ml red wine
400ml chicken or lamb stock
sea salt and black pepper

Heat the oil in a large saucepan over a medium heat, add the diced vegetables and fry for 30–35 minutes, stirring occasionally, until really well coloured, almost black (this is your gravy browning). Add the garlic a few minutes before the end.

Sprinkle over the flour and stir, then gradually add the red wine and cook for a couple of minutes to thicken. Stir in the stock, season and simmer for 5 minutes.

Pass the gravy through a sieve, pressing out as much as possible from the vegetables. If it tastes thin, simmer it for a few minutes, and check the seasoning. Add any juices given out on slicing the loins.

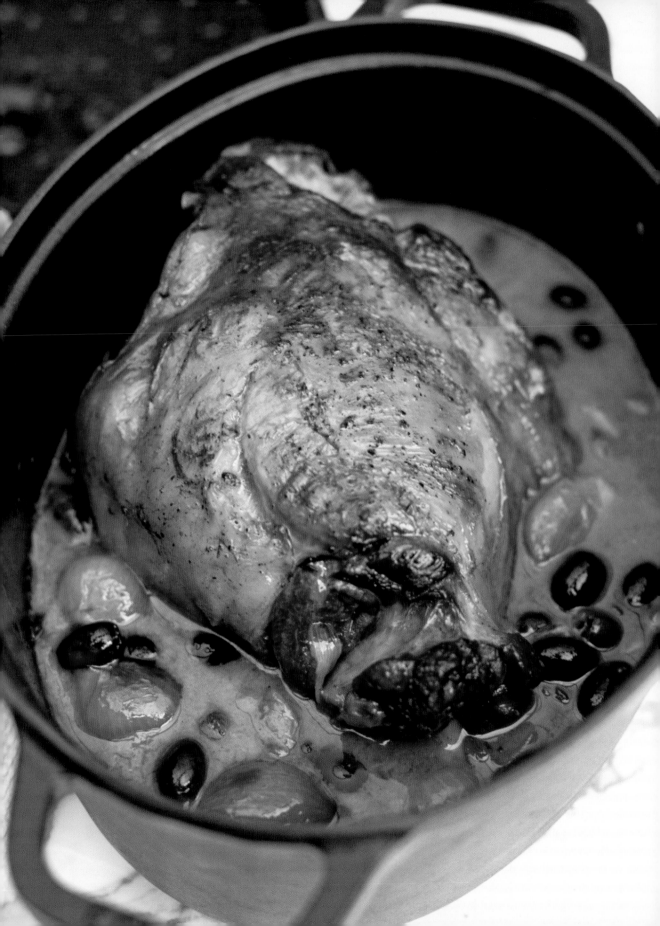

What is it with Christmas and Easter? To whatever extent I mull over the possibility of 'doing things differently for a change', somehow that change never comes. Well, not in my house at any rate, without risk of huge disappointment, and that would never do. Easter lunch has to be lamb. I might just about get away with varying the cut, but only so long as it is roasted; any other contenders to the throne are simply banished with a withering glance.

Actually, this suits me fine. Because this is the best time to be eating British lamb. And I'm not referring to baby pink, forced babes that have never seen the light of day, but lovely mature lamb from the north of the country and the Highlands. This is about the only type that in my eyes matches the superlative esturine lamb in Normandy, whose character comes from being exposed to the weather and having to trudge out to the shore in search of dinner, and then back again to escape the incoming tide. It promises a richer, darker meat that is perfect with the garlic and black olives (see page 202 for suppliers).

Roast leg of lamb with black olives

Serves 6

3 tbsp olive oil
2.7kg leg of lamb
300g shallots, peeled and halved
2 tbsp brandy
10 garlic cloves, peeled

1 beefsteak tomato, skinned, seeded and cut into strips
150ml red wine
sea salt and black pepper
180g black olives, rinsed and pitted

Preheat the oven to 170°C (150°C fan oven) gas mark 4. Heat the olive oil in a large, cast-iron, oval casserole with a lid over a medium-high heat, brown the lamb on all sides and remove. Add the shallots and cook for a few minutes, stirring frequently, until they begin to caramelise.

Return the lamb to the pan, fat-side down, heat the brandy in a ladle and ignite (proximity to a gas flame will do this, or use a match), then pour it over the lamb. If you're unsure about flambéeing, do this 1 tablespoon at a time. Add the garlic, tomato, half the wine and the seasoning, then cover the pan and cook in the oven for 1 hour, turning halfway through.

Add the remaining wine and the olives and return to the oven for 1 hour. Remove the casserole and leave to rest, uncovered, for 15 minutes.

Skim off the surface fat from the casserole and discard the thyme. Carve the lamb and serve with the olives and juices.

I have never subscribed to the fashion for undercooked meats; little makes my heart sink more in a restaurant than to be advised 'We cook the pork (duck, lamb) pink; does madam mind?' To challenge the chef's judgement is never the best foot to put forward, but with a handful of exceptions such as a juicy steak, rare roast beef and venison, in my eyes it is to lose out on meltingly tender roasts, in the company of lots of gravy.

One of the most delicious examples I have had was at the house of a friend, Alex Beard, who braised a leg of lamb in Sauternes, surrounded by an indecent amount of garlic, for five hours. It was so tender that instead of carving the meat he eased it off the bone using a couple of spoons – big steaming chunks of it with lashings of sweet, garlicky gravy. It was hearty, relaxed and bold. In lieu of roast potatoes (a problem with slow-roasts, given that the potatoes need a hot oven) and endless accompaniments, we had thick slices of sourdough bread for scooping it up and a deep bowl of cabbage (see Cabbage with caraway seeds, page 168). I have since successfully reheated a whole leg cooked this way a day or two in advance, so it also joins the list of foods that can be moulded to fit into our lives, rather than the other way around, which is always a cause for celebration.

Monbazillac, Barsac, Sauternes and Jurançon, all contenders, are very sweet wines, but you would never guess it by the end.

Alex Beard's five-hour roast lamb

Serves 6–8

1 onion, peeled
15 cloves
1 small bunch of flat-leaf parsley (about 40g or
    2 packets)
3 sprigs of thyme
2 bay leaves
sea salt and black pepper

1 x 2.5kg leg of lamb, knuckle removed and
    saved
2 tbsp extra virgin olive oil
2 tbsp brandy
5 heads of garlic, cloves peeled and left whole
1 x 75cl bottle Monbazillac, Barsac, Sauternes or
    Jurançon

Use a cast-iron casserole large enough to hold the lamb. Stud the onion with the cloves and place in the casserole with the herbs and some salt, then fill it about half-full with water – it should almost cover the lamb when the meat is immersed later. Bring the liquid to the boil, cover and simmer over a low heat for 20 minutes, then discard the aromatics.

Heat the oven to 130°C (110°C fan oven) gas mark 1. Add the leg of lamb to the casserole and bring the liquid back to the boil, then cover the pan and simmer for another 20 minutes. Drain off and discard the stock and transfer the lamb to a plate – the steam should evaporate within a few minutes. Pat the inside of the casserole dry with kitchen paper, then heat the olive oil in the casserole over a medium heat. Season the lamb and sear to colour it on all sides.

Flambé the lamb with the brandy. If you have a gas hob, the easiest way to do this is to heat the brandy in a ladle until it ignites and then pour it little by little over the lamb, standing well back in case it flares up. Alternatively, just pour it over and let it sizzle for a couple of minutes. Arrange the garlic cloves around or underneath the meat, add the knuckle, pour over the wine and add a little seasoning. Cover the top of the casserole with a double thickness of foil, clamp on the lid and cook in the oven for 5 hours, without disturbing it.

Transfer the leg of lamb to a warm plate, loosely cover with the foil and leave to rest for 20 minutes. Skim any excess fat off the surface of the juices and discard the knuckle. Tip the remaining contents of the casserole into a blender and whizz until smooth (you may need to do this in two goes), then pour back into the casserole and simmer to reduce by about a third. Taste to check the seasoning and pour into a warm jug or gravy boat.

Serve the lamb, pulling it off the bone with a spoon and fork, accompanied by the sauce.

It's the simplicity of this soupy stew that makes it what it is, and there is no point in deviating from the original line-up of potatoes, onions, carrots and lamb, an ultimately soothing ensemble. The only ruse worth heeding is to add the carrots halfway through to avoid overcooking, and to use a combination of maincrop and waxy potatoes, the first to thicken the liquor and the second to provide texture.

Irish stew

Serves 4

1 sprig of rosemary
800g middle neck of lamb chops
3 onions, peeled, halved and sliced
750g floury maincrop potatoes, peeled and
    sliced
sea salt and black pepper

1.2 litres chicken stock
5 large carrots, trimmed, peeled and thickly
    sliced diagonally, stubby ends discarded
400g waxy potatoes, peeled and diced
coarsely chopped flat-leaf parsley, to serve

The rosemary ideally needs to be wrapped in a small square of muslin so that there is no danger of anyone biting on the needles.

Layer the lamb, onions and sliced maincrop potatoes in a large casserole, seasoning the ingredients as you go, and tucking in the rosemary. Pour over the chicken stock and press the ingredients down to submerge them as much as you possibly can; there will probably be a few crags peeking out. Bring to the boil and skim off any foam on the surface, then cover the pan and cook over a low heat for 45 minutes. Stir in the carrots and cook for a further 25 minutes, then add the waxy potatoes and cook for 20 minutes more.

Serve scattered with chopped parsley. The stew can also be made in advance and reheated, in which case you can scrape off the fat on the surface once it has cooled.

I am very fussy about where my sausages come from, and perhaps it is because there is such a chasm between good and bad that there has never been a better time to serve a particularly good sausage with a fanfare when you have friends round (see page 204 for suppliers). When it comes to cooking, I swear by roasting bangers. A proper natural casing caramelises to a lovely sticky gold all over, and the only attention they need is to be turned halfway through.

Sausage and mushroom roast with Stilton-stuffed potatoes

Serves 4

600g medium new or waxy potatoes, scrubbed
sea salt and black pepper
extra virgin olive oil
75g Stilton
8 pork sausages
5 bay leaves

a handful of thyme sprigs
8 portabello or other flat-cap mushrooms,
    stalks trimmed
25g unsalted butter
flat-leaf parsley, coarsely chopped

The potatoes should be roasted and stuffed in advance, and then reheated. Set the oven to 200°C (180°C fan oven) gas mark 6 and bring a large pan of salted water to the boil. Add the potatoes to the pan and cook for 8 minutes, then drain them into a colander. Tip them into a roasting dish that holds them snugly, drizzle over a little olive oil, season with salt and bake for 40–45 minutes, until lightly golden. Remove and leave to cool.

Cut a slit in each potato, to within 1cm of the ends, and fill with a sliver of cheese.

Heat the oven to 200°C (180°C fan oven) gas mark 6, arrange the sausages in a large roasting dish and then cook in the oven for 20 minutes.

Take out of the oven, turn the sausages and place the bay, thyme and mushrooms in between them. Drizzle over some olive oil, season and pop a sliver of butter into each mushroom cup. Return to the oven for another 25 minutes, adding the potatoes to reheat 10 minutes before the end. Serve scattered with parsley.

Both loin and belly slow-roast beautifully, the latter being that much more economical. You can roast the belly on the bone, and if it is loin then ask your butcher for the row of chine bones at the base to be removed – you can roast these alongside the joint. Also ask for the rind to be sliced off – so the fat is evenly distributed between meat and skin – and scored. The Cabbage with caraway seeds on page 168 could be delicious with this.

Spiced, slow-roast pork with orange

Serves 6

I tsp ground cumin	I orange
I tsp ground coriander	5 red onions, peeled and quartered
sea salt and black pepper	I tbsp dark muscovado sugar
I x 2.2–2.5kg pork loin rib or belly roast	100ml dry white wine
2 tbsp groundnut oil	150ml water

Heat the oven to 200°C (180°C fan oven) gas mark 6. Combine the cumin and coriander with ½ teaspoon of salt in a small bowl and rub all over the pork flesh. Heat the groundnut oil over a medium heat in a roasting dish that will hold the joint with a couple of inches around the side to spare, and sear the pork to colour on all sides. Place it fat-side up with the chine bones to the side if you are roasting a loin, turn the oven down to 160°C (140°C fan oven) gas mark 3, and roast for 1 hour. At the same time roast the crackling. Rub some salt into the pork skin, place it skin-up in a small roasting dish and then place in the oven.

After 1 hour, using a potato peeler, remove the orange zest from the fruit in wide strips. Scatter the onions and orange strips around the joint, sprinkle over the sugar, baste them and return to the oven to cook for a further 1½ hours. Shortly thereafter you will find that the joint and onions are sitting in copious pan juices. Baste the onions a couple of times more in the process of roasting, but don't baste the pork or crackling.

Remove the roast to a warm plate, surround it with the onions and discard the chine bones and orange zest. Cover with foil and leave to rest for 20 minutes. Turn the oven up to 220°C (200°C fan oven) gas mark 7 and continue to roast the crackling while the joint is resting. It should crisp and turn pale with small bubbles below the surface.

To make the gravy, skim the fat off the roasting tray, add the wine and simmer to reduce by half, then add the water and continue to cook for a few minutes longer. Strain it into a warm jug.

Carve the roast – you should get one slice between each rib and one with the bone in. Drain any fat from the crackling into a small bowl – you can keep it for roasting potatoes and cooking the cabbage. Serve the roast pork and onions with the crackling and gravy.

A braised, boned gammon offers up beautifully succulent, thick, pink slabs of meat. I'd opt for an unsmoked or green joint, so that any liquor used in making a béchamel to go with it is clean in flavour, and that goes for any soups, too, that derive from the stock.

In recent years, though, I have been disappointed with some cures from quite reputable sources, which have been so mild as to be almost imperceptible. There is little worse than cooking a ham only to find it has the colour and flavour of roast pork – I like a definite salty bite to mine. Not all hams will require soaking, and for this I would be advised by the butcher, who may in any case have cured the gammon inhouse and know exactly how salty it is. That said, there is less call to soak a joint that is to be braised, where some of the salt will leach into the water, than there is for gammon destined to be roasted or baked, where the juices will concentrate during cooking.

Braised ham with a fondue sauce and roast onions

Serves 6–8

For the ham

1 x 2kg unsmoked gammon, boned and rolled

3 outer sticks of celery, trimmed
  and sliced

2 carrots, trimmed and sliced

1 leek, trimmed and sliced

2 bay leaves

50g dark muscovado sugar

For the sauce

50g unsalted butter

40g plain flour

150g crème fraîche

1 tsp Dijon mustard

120g grated mature Cheddar

black pepper

For the onions

2kg red and white onions, unpeeled

unsalted butter, to serve

Place the gammon in a large saucepan, cover with cold water and bring to the boil. Discard the water and start again with fresh water to cover, adding the vegetables and bay leaves. Bring to the boil, then simmer gently for 1½ hours.

Towards the end of this time, heat the oven to 200°C (180°C fan oven) gas mark 6. About 10 minutes before the ham is ready, put the onions on a tray and into the oven and bake for 1 hour.

Using two forks, transfer the ham from the pan onto a board. Reserve the stock. Remove any string and paper from the ham, pull off the rind and press the sugar evenly over the fat. Place the ham in a roasting tray and pour 2–3mm of the stock into the base. Roast for 20–30 minutes until the fat has a mahogany hue. Transfer the ham to a warm serving plate and let it rest for 20 minutes while you make the sauce.

Melt the butter in a small, non-stick saucepan. Stir in the flour and allow the roux to seethe for about a minute. Working off the heat, gradually incorporate 400ml of the ham stock. Bring the sauce to the boil, stirring constantly, then whisk in the crème fraîche and mustard and simmer over a low heat for 10 minutes, stirring occasionally. Add the cheese and whisk until it melts, then season with black pepper.

Carve the ham and serve on warm plates with the sauce spooned over it, and the onions in their skins, slit open and dotted with butter.

Many will be familiar with roasting a sea bass or chicken in a crust of salt as a means of sealing in the succulence and flavour. A salt crust for ham would be coals to Newcastle, but excellent results can be obtained by enveloping a ham in a paste made of flour and water, and it's a lovely, messy, hands-on affair.

Parsley purée goes magestically with ham. Take 400g flat-leaf parsley leaves and stalks, trim the ends and cut into lengths. Boil the parsley for 3 minutes, then drain. Blend in a liquidiser with 40g unsalted butter, some seasoning and a squeeze of lemon juice, adding a drop of water to get it going if necessary. If making in advance, add the lemon juice at the last minute before serving. Serve hot or cold.

Ham baked in a crust

Serves 8–10

For the ham

1 x 3.5–4.5kg smoked or unsmoked knuckle-end gammon joint on the bone

750g plain flour

650ml water

125g fresh sourdough or brown breadcrumbs (see page 62)

1–2 tbsp black peppercorns

Soak the gammon in cold water overnight, then remove. Heat the oven to 190°C (170°C fan oven) gas mark 5. Line a large roasting tray with foil.

Place the flour in a large bowl and stir in the water in a few goes to make a sticky paste. Using your fingers, coat the cut-side of the ham with paste to 1cm thick and place this side downwards on the foil-lined tray, then coat the skin. The gammon needs to bake for 50 minutes per kilo, so calculate accordingly. After 10–15 minutes in the oven, once the paste has begun to dry out, remove the joint and patch any bald spots with paste that has slipped down. Once cooked, leave the ham to cool for about 30 minutes.

Spread the breadcrumbs in a thin layer on the base of a couple of roasting or baking trays and toast for about 9 minutes until lightly golden. Whizz them in a food processor, then transfer to a bowl. Place the peppercorns (the amount depends on how peppery you want the crust) in a coffee grinder and give them a whizz, stopping short of a powder. Combine with the breadcrumbs.

Lift the crust off the sides of the ham in pieces, then transfer the joint to a board, knuckle up. Slice or pull off the rind, leaving as much fat as possible.

Using your fingers, coat the ham with the breadcrumb mixture, pressing the crumbs down firmly to cover it as generously as possible. Place it on a clean plate, again knuckle upwards, and leave it to cool completely. It can then be turned on its side, ready to carve and serve.

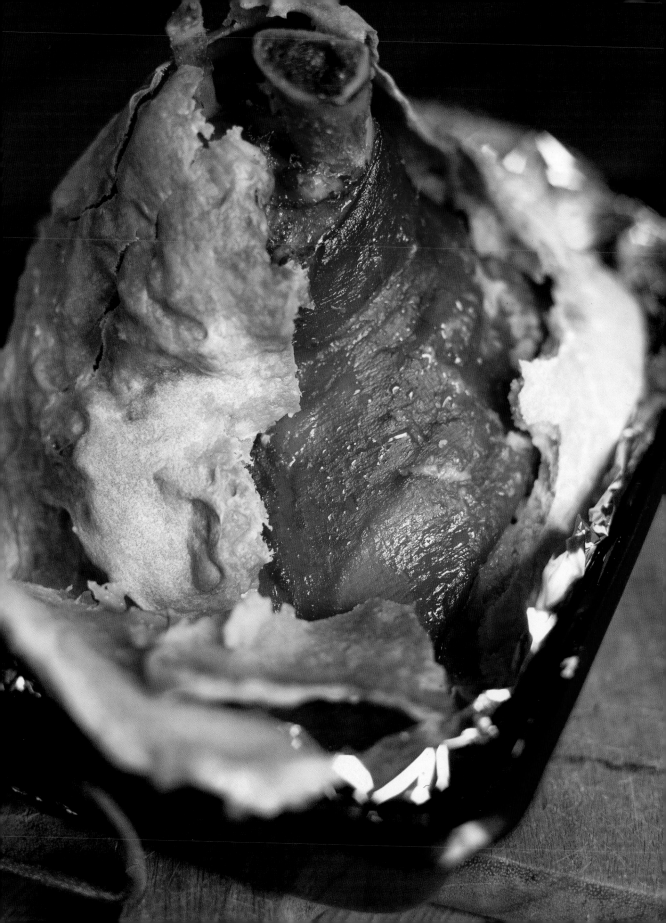

RAGU

I nearly always traipse to the local butcher or farmers' market on a Saturday morning for the Sunday roast, and buy some beef or lamb mince while I am there. Its long, slow simmering makes a pleasant Sunday evening's cooking – nothing too demanding in the way of attention: you can pop back to the stove and add a little more stock every now and again in between rustling up the homework and gym bags for Monday morning. It's an insurance against the inevitable stress of the weekdays to follow; you can serve it with pasta or rice on Monday, and turn the remainder into a cottage pie, lasagne, or moussaka for Wednesday or Thursday, and half the work's done.

Despite the very British nature of the ingredients that go into a ragú, it is the Italians who have the patience to elicit the best from them. A properly made ragú takes a minimum of two hours' simmering, the first stage is like making any savoury mince, and you could, if time is tight, stop there. But the finesse comes with the second stage of cooking, where it is simmered with the addition of some stock now and again, which builds in a richness of flavour and affords it a more luxurious texture.

And if you're entertaining or having people to stay, then it's probably just what your friends feel like eating. When you live in the country and visitors have to drive for hours to reach you, little is worse than being met by the latest experimental trend, when all you want is the familiarity and comfort of a cottage pie and a glass of red wine. It goes without saying that you can, of course, also just ladle this over pasta and shower it with Parmesan cheese. Heaven.

The real ragú

Serves 4–6

1 carrot, trimmed and peeled
1 stick of celery, trimmed
1 onion, peeled
25g unsalted butter, plus 10g
1 tbsp extra virgin olive oil
2 tbsp fresh oregano or marjoram leaves
800g minced beef

150ml full-cream milk
150ml red wine
1 x 400g tin chopped tomatoes
1 small dried red chilli, finely chopped
sea salt
425–600ml chicken or beef stock

Cut the carrot, celery and onion into chunks, place in a food processor and chop finely. Heat the 25g of butter and the olive oil in a medium saucepan over a medium heat, add the chopped vegetables and oregano or marjoram and sweat for about 5 minutes, stirring occasionally until softened.

Add the meat, turn the heat up and cook, stirring until it changes colour. Now add the milk 2 tablespoons at a time, cooking each addition until it's absorbed.

Pour in the red wine, boil until reduced by half, then turn the heat down. Add the tomatoes and chilli and season with salt. Simmer over the very lowest heat for about an hour, stirring occasionally, until all the juices have been absorbed. Keep a careful eye on it towards the end to prevent it from burning. Tip the pan and skim off any surface fat.

The ragú needs to cook very slowly for another hour. Add the stock about 150ml at a time, adding more if needed. Cook until each batch is reduced to about half. The end result should be rich and soupy. If necessary, skim it again and taste for seasoning.

Most lasagne sheets can be layered in their dry state without prior boiling. But for the pasta to absorb liquid and emerge juicy and succulent, this does demand a sea of very thin béchamel and a soupy ragú.

Lasagne al forno

Serves 6

1 x recipe for Ragú (see page 81)
100g freshly grated Parmesan
200–300g (12–18 15cm x 8cm sheets) dried
    yellow or green lasagne

For the béchamel
50g unsalted butter
40g plain flour
1 litre full-cream milk
1 bay leaf
freshly grated nutmeg
sea salt

To make the béchamel, melt the butter in a medium saucepan, stir in the flour and let the roux seethe for about a minute. Off the heat, gradually incorporate the milk – slowly to begin with. Add the bay leaf, bring it to a simmer, stirring occasionally, then cook over a low heat for 10 minutes. Give it an occasional stir to make sure it doesn't catch on the bottom. Season with nutmeg and salt.

Select a 30cm x 20cm x 6cm baking dish and layer the ingredients as follows: cover the base of the dish with a thin layer of ragú, then drizzle over some béchamel. Scatter over a little Parmesan, then cover with a layer of lasagne, breaking the sheets to fit if necessary. Repeat until all the ingredients are used up, ending with ragú, béchamel and whatever Parmesan is left. In total you should have four layers of pasta and five of ragú and béchamel. At this point you can cover and chill the lasagne for up to 12 hours.

When ready to cook, heat the oven to 190°C (170°C fan oven) gas mark 5, and bake the lasagne for 30–35 minutes until golden and bubbling on the surface.

Cottage pie, sizzling from the oven, is the ultimate comfort food to welcome home the family or winter visitors. A big pan of roasted parsnips and perhaps some sautéed wild mushrooms are ideal serving partners.

Cottage pie

Serves 6

1 x recipe for Ragú (see page 81)

For the mash
1.3kg maincrop potatoes, peeled and halved or
    quartered if large

120g unsalted butter, diced, plus an extra knob
sea salt and black pepper

For the mash, either steam the potatoes in the top half of a steamer set over simmering water in the lower half, or bring a large pan of salted water to the boil, add the potatoes, bring back to a simmer and cook until tender. Drain them into a sieve or a colander and leave for a minute or two for any surface moisture to evaporate, then pass through a mouli-légumes or a sieve back into the pan. Add the 120g butter and plenty of salt and black pepper.

Transfer the ragú to six shallow ovenproof dishes, discarding the herbs. Spread the potato generously over the surface of each to allow for plenty of crispy golden topping and fork into a crisscross of furrows. You can prepare the dish to this point in advance, then simply cover and chill until required.

When ready to cook, heat the oven to 200°C (180°C fan oven) gas mark 6, dot the surface of the potato with the remaining butter and cook for 30–40 minutes until sizzling and golden brown on top.

Morels can be put to good use here, especially the dried ones, where the soaking liquor can be used to braise the beef. Fresh mushrooms are also a delight, in which case use 300g in all – you may like to mix a few wild ones in with some flavourful cultivated ones.

Pot-roast beef with mushrooms

Serves 4

For the roast beef
30g dried morels
1½ tbsp vegetable oil
sea salt and black pepper
1kg joint of topside beef
75ml Madeira
125ml mushroom soaking liquor or water

1 bay leaf
5 sprigs of thyme, tied into a bundle with string
½ tsp each plain flour and unsalted butter, blended
200g wild or flavourful cultivated mushrooms, picked over and sliced if necessary
Parmesan Yorkshires, to serve (see page 89)

Place the dried mushrooms in a bowl, just cover with boiling water and leave to soak for 15 minutes. Drain them, reserving the liquor, and halve any large mushrooms.

Heat ½ tablespoon of the vegetable oil in a cast-iron casserole over a medium-high heat. Season the joint and sear to colour it all over. Take your time doing this as it is the only browning the meat will get. Transfer the joint to a plate and tip out the fat, then return the joint to the casserole.

Pour over the Madeira and the mushroom-soaking liquor, discarding the last little gritty bit, or water. Add the bay leaf and thyme. Bring the liquid to a simmer, cover the pan and cook over a low heat for 35 minutes. Remove the joint, place on a warm plate and leave it to rest for 15 minutes.

Skim any fat off the surface of the cooking juices and discard the herbs. Add the flour and butter paste in small pieces, blend into the juices and simmer for a few minutes until it thickens into a rich gravy. Taste for seasoning.

Heat the remaining tablespoon of vegetable oil in a large frying pan over a medium-high heat, add the fresh and dried mushrooms and sauté for a few minutes until soft, seasoning them towards the end. If they give out any liquid, turn the heat up and continue to cook until this evaporates.

Carve the beef, adding any juices given out to the sauce. Serve the beef with the mushrooms to the side, the gravy spooned over it and accompanied by the Parmesan Yorkshires.

YORKSHIRE PUDDING

Yorkshire pudding had its finest hour when meat was roasted on a spit and the pudding would bake beneath it, absorbing all the dripping and meaty juices as it did so. While we are no longer in the habit of roasting our meat like this, there is no doubt that Yorkshire pudding not only welcomes gravy but cries out for it. On its own it is about as exciting as a pancake without lemon juice or sugar.

Making the batter

I like my Yorkshire puddings to be golden, risen and crusty – insignificant puffs that can be eaten in quantity. I find by far the most effective way of preparing a lump-free batter is to place all the ingredients in a liquidiser and blend them until smooth and creamy. You can also use a hand-held electric whisk. Though to prepare the batter by hand the good old-fashioned way, place the dry ingredients in a bowl. Break in the eggs and roughly mix them in, then start to add the liquid a little at a time, smoothing the mixture with a wooden spoon. If at the end the mixture appears at all lumpy you can whisk it for good measure.

Parmesan Yorkshires

Makes 9–12

50g plain flour, sifted
½ tsp sea salt
I medium egg
75ml full-cream milk

75ml water
vegetable oil
25g freshly grated Parmesan

Place the flour, salt, egg, milk and water in a liquidiser and blend until smooth and creamy. You can also use a hand-held electric whisk. Leave the batter to rest for 30 minutes.

Preheat the oven to 220°C (200°C fan oven) gas mark 7. Liberally brush the inside of a tray of fairy cake moulds with vegetable oil and place in the oven to heat for 10 minutes. Either rewhisk or blend the batter and stir in the Parmesan.

Fill the fairy cake moulds two-thirds full with the mixture and bake for 15–20 minutes until golden and risen. If you have cooked the Yorkshires in advance, return them to the oven to heat through about 5 minutes before eating.

Oxtail is back from the cold as one of several slow-cooking cuts that are regaining their popularity. It is a matter of some wonder that anything so humble can be elevated to something sublime, and merely with the passage of time. My poor mother must have felt less than flattered when as children we referred to her many casseroles as 'rotten wood', but when I'm slow-cooking beef and lamb, that is exactly the texture I am aiming for: something that literally falls apart on the fork.

Most butchers will be able to provide you with oxtail, though it's worth a phone call a couple of days in advance to make sure they set some aside. You need good-sized joints; the last few tapered sections of the tail are fine for stock, but don't have any meat on them to speak of. Or you could substitute any other cut of braising steak if you prefer. My butcher swears by top rump, and Donald Russell (see Suppliers, page 203) sells rib trim, which is a classic daube cut. In this case you can reduce the cooking time to a couple of hours. The accompanying carbohydrate of choice has to be either buttery boiled potatoes or champ.

Braised oxtail and onions

Serves 6

150ml Madeira or medium sherry
2 garlic cloves, peeled and crushed to a paste
a few sprigs of thyme
1 bay leaf, torn into pieces
¼ tsp ground cinnamon
¼ tsp ground nutmeg
2kg oxtail, separated into joints
sea salt and black pepper

extra virgin olive oil
600g onions, peeled, halved and sliced
1 bottle red wine
300g small chestnut or button mushrooms,
    stalks trimmed
4 tbsp chopped flat-leaf parsley mixed with
    finely grated zest of 1 orange, to serve

It isn't essential to marinate the meat, but it does give it that extra something. Combine the Madeira or sherry, the garlic, thyme, bay leaf and spices in a large bowl. Add the meat and baste it, then cover and chill for about 6 hours or overnight, basting it halfway through if you remember.

Remove the meat from the marinade, dry it and season. Reserve the marinade. Heat 1 tablespoon of olive oil in a large frying pan over a highish heat, add half the meat and sear to colour it on all sides. Remove it and sear the remainder in the same way.

Heat a couple of tablespoons of olive oil in a large casserole over a medium-high heat, add the onions and cook for 10–15 minutes until golden, stirring occasionally. Add the marinade, the wine and some seasoning, and then the browned oxtail. Bring to the boil, then cover the pan and simmer over a low heat for 2 hours, giving it a stir halfway through.

Heat a couple of tablespoons of olive oil in a large frying pan over a medium-high heat, add the mushrooms, season them and sauté for a few minutes until lightly coloured. Stir these into the casserole and simmer for another hour until the meat is fork-tender.

Transfer the meat and mushrooms to a bowl and simmer the juices to reduce them by about a third, discarding the herbs. Return the meat and mushrooms to the gravy. Serve scattered with the chopped parsley and orange and accompanied by Champ (see page 169).

When eating oxtail, I enjoy sifting through the oxtail bones and prising succulent morsels off them, much as I do with a fish stew. But for those who don't, another great way of serving oxtail is to remove the meat from the bone and bake it covered with a silky mash, for a seriously good cottage pie.

Oxtail cottage pie

Serves 6

1 x recipe for Braised oxtail (see page 91)
1.3kg floury maincrop potatoes, peeled and
   halved or quartered if large
120g unsalted butter

3 tbsp full-cream milk
sea salt and black pepper
50g white breadcrumbs (see page 62)
1 tbsp vegetable oil

Make the oxtail casserole, omitting the mushrooms. Leave it to cool, then remove the meat from the bones, shred it with your fingers and add enough of the onion gravy to moisten it. Reserve the rest.

For the mash, either steam the potatoes in the top half of a steamer set over simmering water in the lower half, or bring a large pan of salted water to the boil, add the potatoes, bring back to a simmer and cook until tender. Drain them into a sieve or a colander and leave for a minute or two for any surface moisture to evaporate, then pass through a mouli-légumes or a sieve back into the pan. Add the butter and, once this has melted, the milk and plenty of seasoning. Mix thoroughly to a smooth mash.

Spoon the oxtail into a baking dish, then smooth the mashed potato on top. Toss the breadcrumbs with the vegetable oil and scatter them over the potato. The pie can be prepared up to this point in advance.

When ready to cook, heat the oven to 200°C (180°C fan oven) gas mark 6. Bake the pie for 30–35 minutes.

Reheat the remaining onion gravy and serve together with the pie.

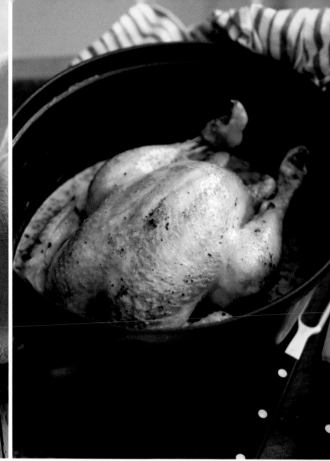

4

Poultry

The recipe for these chicken wings was created by our family friend Jean-Christophe Chavaillard and has become a firm barbecue favourite. My eight-year-old son, Louis, would swim oceans for a plateful.

Sticky chicken wings

Makes 12

For the marinade
4 tbsp extra virgin olive oil
1 tbsp finely chopped rosemary
1 tbsp finely chopped thyme
2 bay leaves, torn into pieces
3 garlic cloves, peeled and crushed to
    a paste

For the chicken
12 chicken wings
1 tbsp Dijon mustard
1 tbsp runny honey
sea salt and black pepper

Combine the ingredients for the marinade in a large bowl. Add the chicken wings, coating them in the mixture, then cover and chill overnight.

Blend the mustard and honey in a small bowl. Turn the chicken wings in their marinade, then season them.

Outdoors: Barbecue the wings for 10–15 minutes until they seem half cooked, turning them once, then brush on both sides with the mustard-honey baste and cook for approximately 10 minutes more (again turning them once), until golden.

Indoors: Heat the oven to 240°C (220°C fan oven) gas mark 9. Season the chicken wings on both sides, arrange them skin-side up in a roasting dish and place in the oven for 15 minutes until they start to colour. Next, brush both the lower and top side of the wings with the mustard-honey mixture and roast for another 10–15 minutes until golden.

A roast chicken, for me, epitomises the concept of cooking today with tomorrow in mind. And to this end I'm going to suggest you roast a couple of chickens rather than just the one next Sunday (unless that is you are two in number). The idea is that having had your fill of that top slice of breast with its golden skin, and a few silky shreds of wing or leg, there will still be plenty for a Bang Bang chicken salad in a few days' time, as well as the stock for some soups or stews.

Cutting the vegetables into thin strips gives this salad an ethereal air. But don't be put off if you're in a rush – simply slice the vegetables any way you like.

Bang Bang chicken salad

Serves 6

For the dressing
200g smooth peanut butter
4 tbsp sesame oil
3 tbsp vegetable oil
2 tbsp sweet chilli sauce
2 tbsp lime juice
½ tsp cayenne pepper
sea salt

For the salad
1 tbsp sesame seeds
1 cucumber, peeled, quartered, deseeded and cut into thin strips 5–8cm long
4 medium-sized carrots, trimmed, peeled and cut into thin strips 5–8cm long
100g sprouting seeds or beansprouts
4 spring onions, trimmed and cut into thin strips about 5cm long
a generous squeeze of lime juice
450–500g cooked chicken, shredded

To make the dressing, gently warm the peanut butter in a bowl set over a pan of simmering water, stirring occasionally, until it melts. Stir in the oils, then the chilli sauce, lime juice and cayenne and taste for seasoning. Leave this to cool to room temperature. If it gets too cold it will start to firm up again, in which case it can be gently rewarmed in a bowl over simmering water until it thins to the right consistency.

To make the salad, toast the sesame seeds in a frying pan until a pale gold, then transfer to a bowl to cool. Combine all the vegetables in a bowl. You can prepare everything to this point in advance.

Just before eating, toss the vegetables with a squeeze of lime juice and a little salt, and mix with the chicken. Drizzle the dressing over and scatter with the sesame seeds.

This is a great picnic favourite of mine. It's curious how removing dishes from their usual context imbues them with an unaccustomed glamour – I can only say how very good this bird tastes out of doors. Swaddled in foil the minute it comes out of the oven, it oozes buttery saffron-scented juices as you mosey to your destination, collecting them in a tantalising little pool at the base, which together with its wrinkled golden skin is an invitation a crust of bread can't refuse. And it should still be warm, an hour or so later, when you spread yourselves out on rugs.

For a crowd of people you want a really big, fat bird resting on its haunches. Alternatively, double up and roast two.

Butter-roasted saffron chicken

Serves 6

a good pinch of ground saffron (about
    25 filaments)
1 tbsp thyme leaves
sea salt

75g unsalted butter, softened
1 x 2kg chicken
juice of 1 lemon
cayenne pepper

Heat the oven to 220°C (200°C fan oven) gas mark 7.

Blend the ground saffron, thyme and a little salt with 50g of the butter. Don't worry if the saffron disappears into the butter at this stage, it will make its presence felt as the bird roasts. Starting at the neck end of the chicken, slip your fingers beneath the skin to loosen it either side of the breastbone. Then spread the butter over the breast meat and pat the skin back into place, smoothing the butter out evenly. Place the chicken in a roasting dish, rub with the remaining butter, pour over the lemon juice, season with salt and dust with cayenne pepper.

Roast the chicken for 1 hour, without basting, then transfer it to a plate, tipping any juices inside into the roasting dish. Pour these into a bowl or jug straight away and leave the chicken to rest for 20 minutes.

Serve the chicken hot or cold, with the buttery juices spooned over for those who like them, though you could skim off the butter if you prefer.

A part of me feels I am being disloyal to potato farmers when I start extolling the wonders of rice, not least because of how far afield it comes from. But then I remember that Europe too has a thriving tradition – that of Italy and Spain goes back hundreds of years. Prior to the twentieth century we did precious little with rice except make pottage and puds – our take on the starchy short-grain varieties, while its recent coming of age has centred on long-grain types.

The name that has really taken us by storm is basmati (and there are some eight thousand varieties); it's up there as the perfect all-rounder. It helps that both my children adore it, in fact I can't think of many children who don't. Not that they appreciate its finer points (the particular scent that comes with its provenance in the foothills of the Himalayas), they just know it tastes good.

This is one of my stock weekday pilafs. My butcher sells the most luxurious deep-pink lobed chicken livers, fresh rather than frozen, which makes all the difference.

Chicken liver pilaf with pistachios

Serves 4

500g chicken livers
2 tbsp olive oil
sea salt and black pepper
3 unsmoked streaky bacon rashers (rind
  removed), diced
I white or yellow onion, peeled, halved and
  sliced
225g basmati rice, soaked for 30 minutes in cold
  water and drained, or rinsed in a sieve

I bay leaf
2 sprigs of thyme
2 x 5cm strips of lemon zest
150ml dry white wine
300ml chicken stock
3 tbsp coarsely chopped flat-leaf parsley
75g roasted and salted pistachios, shelled and
  coarsely chopped
hot and spicy chutney, to serve

Cut the central fatty membranes out of the chicken livers, leaving the lobes as whole as possible.
You will need to cook the livers in two goes. Heat 1 tablespoon of the olive oil in a large frying
pan over a medium-high heat, add half the livers, season and sear briefly to colour on both
sides, leaving them as uncooked and bloody in the middle as possible, then remove to a bowl.
Once you have cooked and removed the second batch, add the bacon and fry, stirring
occasionally until nicely coloured. Put to one side with the chicken livers.

Heat the remaining olive oil in a medium saucepan over a medium heat, add the onion
and sweat for 8–10 minutes, stirring occasionally, until soft and lightly coloured.

Add the rice, bay leaf, thyme and lemon zest and stir to coat in the oil. Pour in the wine
and stock and season generously. Bring the liquid to the boil, cover with a tight-fitting lid and
simmer over a low heat for 8 minutes, adding the chicken livers and bacon halfway through.
Then, without removing the lid, turn the heat off and leave the pilaf for 15 minutes to dry out
further, when it will also become more tender.

Give it a stir to fluff up the rice, and remove the herbs and zest. Toss in the parsley and
pistachios and serve with chutney.

The French have long made an art form out of poaching a whole chicken. In times past, a 'poule au pot' was a farmer's wife's parsimonious means of making use of a laying chicken who was past her best and would be tough roasted. But if simmered long and slow enough in the pot it would be adequately tenderised, and also produce the proceeds for a week of soups. Often chickens cooked this way are smothered with a rich sauce, at times just pure untreated cream, heated and poured over. Plenty would argue that anything tastes good with that kind of treatment, and certainly I would part company with the French in their adoration of poules, as I have yet to eat a succulent bird. An ordinary roasting bird, however, cooks in a fraction of the time and emerges from the pan beautifully succulent and tender, although the resulting stock is weaker.

Still, you have the beginnings of a stock. Having carved your chicken, skim the cooking liquor, pop the carcass into the pot and simmer for an hour. For a richer stock, simply cook to reduce it further. You can also use the liquid for cooking potatoes or rice to go with the bird, and I like to cook haricot beans alongside the chicken, which soak up the flavours. This is a dish where all the ingredients work to influence each other: the chicken and vegetables flavour the broth, which flavours the haricot beans.

Chicken in a pot

Serves 4

200g dried haricot beans, soaked overnight
2 heads of garlic, cloves peeled
2 carrots, peeled and thickly sliced
2 sticks of celery, trimmed and thickly sliced
2 bay leaves
5 sprigs of thyme
150ml dry white wine
2.5 litres water

sea salt and black pepper
1.6kg chicken, untrussed
250g French beans, topped and tailed
7 tbsp extra virgin olive oil, plus a little extra
1 tsp truffle oil (optional)
3 slices of air-dried ham, cut into strips
coarsely chopped flat-leaf parsley, to serve

Drain the haricot beans and put them in a pan with enough water to cover by about 3cm. Bring to the boil, then turn down the heat and simmer for 15 minutes. Drain.

Place the garlic, carrots, celery, bay leaves and thyme in a large, cast-iron casserole that will fit the chicken with some room to spare. Pour in the wine and water, add 1½ teaspoons of salt and some black pepper and bring to the boil. Place the chicken in the pot, then sprinkle the haricot beans around it. The water should almost cover the chicken, so add more if necessary. Return to the boil, then cover the pan and poach over a low heat for 50 minutes. Towards the end of cooking, bring a pan of salted water to the boil for the French beans.

Transfer the chicken to a plate and leave to rest for 20 minutes. Continue to cook the haricot beans at a rapid boil for another 15 minutes: don't worry if they don't seem as tender as normal (the salt toughens the skins), as all will be well when the purée is sieved.

About 5 minutes before serving, add the French beans to the boiling water and cook until just tender. Drain and return to the pan, then toss with 1 tablespoon of the olive oil, the truffle oil if using, and a little seasoning, then mix in the strips of ham.

Drain the haricot beans and vegetables into a sieve, then discard the herbs and all but a few pieces of carrot. Add the beans and remaining vegetables to a blender and purée with 6 tablespoons of the olive oil, 100ml of cooking liquor and a little salt. Pass the purée through a sieve into a small saucepan and gently reheat.

Carve the chicken and serve on a bed of bean purée on warm plates. Drizzle with a little olive oil, scatter with parsley and serve with the French beans.

Enriching a broth with mayonnaise is typical of a bourride, but do try this variation with chicken, which is equally successful. This recipe makes more mayonnaise than you are likely to want, but it has plenty of uses. An exotic egg mayonnaise sandwich, perhaps, with roasted red onions and watercress.

Poached chicken with saffron mayonnaise

Serves 4

For the mayonnaise
a pinch of saffron filaments (about 20)
I medium egg yolk, at room temperature
I tsp Dijon mustard
sea salt
200ml groundnut or vegetable oil
I tbsp extra virgin olive oil
a squeeze of lemon juice

For the soup
750ml chicken stock
100ml dry white wine
I tsp thyme leaves
I head of garlic, cloves peeled
3 small heads of pak choi, damaged leaves
    discarded
2 skinless chicken breasts
100g baby spinach leaves
3 spring onions, trimmed and finely sliced

Grind the saffron filaments in a pestle and mortar, pour over a teaspoon of boiling water and leave to infuse for 15 minutes. Place the egg yolk in a bowl with the mustard and a pinch of salt and whisk to blend them. Now start to whisk in the groundnut or vegetable oil, a trickle at a time, until you can see the sauce thickening, then add in bolder streams, adding the extra virgin olive oil at the end. Whisk in the saffron infusion and a squeeze of lemon juice. Cover and chill until required.

To make the soup, bring the stock and wine to the boil in a large saucepan with the thyme, garlic and some salt, then simmer for 15 minutes.

Separate the pak choi leaves and cut the large outer ones in half lengthways. Cut out the tendon on the base of the chicken breasts if apparent. Season the chicken breasts with salt, add to the broth, cover and poach for another 15 minutes, turning them halfway through if not completely submerged.

Transfer the chicken to a plate to rest for 5 minutes. Add the pak choi to the pan and poach for 5 minutes, or until just tender, adding the spinach a minute or two before the end. Taste for seasoning.

Ladle the soup and vegetables into four warm bowls. Slice the chicken downwards across the grain and place a few slices in the centre of each bowl. Dollop the mayonnaise on top and scatter with spring onions.

A tale of this dish begins at dawn one morning after an overnight ferry crossing to the Continent, which as many will know leaves you feeling more frazzled than when you set off on holiday. But to soothe some of those nerves the local market was at least in full swing in the half-light, and after securing a fine-looking chicken, a bunch of hardy herbs and another of watercress, some potatoes, a slice of fresh, handmade butter and a tub of raw cream, the stress of the crossing gave way to the promise of the dinner that lay ahead. This was without bargaining with the conditions in the kitchen of the little cottage we had rented – its flimsy plastic table that served as a country dining table and rocked precariously if you did more than look at it, and which also served as the kitchen worksurface, and an oven that shuddered alarmingly as it was turned on. I looked instead to the hob, and there was at least a casserole and a knife of sorts.

Dinner that night, even allowing for our exhaustion, was sublime. Having coloured the bird all over I popped it into a casserole, tipped in a glass of wine, tucked a bay leaf and a couple of sprigs of thyme to its side, clamped the lid on and left it alone for an hour. In the meantime, I boiled up some potatoes and threw a hefty lump of salted butter into their floury midst. And once the bird was cooked, removed it and stirred the tub of raw cream and a large pile of coarsely chopped watercress into the casserole. My mouth still waters at the thought of that succulent chicken with its rich creamy green sauce and the buttery potatoes mashed into it.

Pot-roast chicken with watercress sauce

Serves 4

1.6kg chicken, untrussed
vegetable oil
sea salt and black pepper
2 bay leaves
3 sprigs of thyme
150ml dry white wine

1 tsp each plain flour and unsalted butter,
  blended
1 bunch of watercress (about 100g),
  trimmed and chopped
200ml crème fraîche

Coat the chicken all over with oil and season it. Heat a frying pan over a medium-high heat, add the chicken and sear to colour it thoroughly to a deep gold on all sides. Place it breast-side up in a large, cast-iron casserole. Add the herbs and the wine, bring to a simmer, then cover and cook over a low heat for 55 minutes.

Uncover the chicken and leave it to rest in the pan for 15 minutes. Remove it to a plate, pouring any juices inside back into the pan, and carve it into hearty chunks.

Skim any excess fat off the juices in the pan and remove the herbs. Bring back to the boil, then add the butter and flour paste in small pieces and stir until it has melted. Stir in the watercress and the crème fraîche and taste for seasoning. Allow this to heat through, then serve poured over the chicken.

Proper pies involve a fair bit of work, but are well worth the effort. Few dishes allow you to relax before the meal as well as after, so a pie is great for entertaining, scoring highly in the sociability stakes. Use nice meaty mushrooms that will hold their shape – wild varieties are unbeatable for flavour. Serve the pie with a pot of mash and a buttery mélange of peas, beans, sugar snaps and mangetout.

Chicken and mushroom pie

Serves 6

For the pastry
225g unsalted butter, diced
350g plain flour, plus extra for dusting
sea salt
1 medium egg
1 egg yolk blended with 1 tbsp milk

For the filling
80g unsalted butter
45g plain flour
300ml jellied or strong chicken stock
200ml crème fraîche

black pepper
1 heaped tsp Dijon mustard
2 tsp finely chopped tarragon leaves
2 tbsp extra virgin olive oil
2 shallots, peeled and finely chopped
2 garlic cloves, peeled and finely chopped
400g mushrooms, wild and cultivated,
    trimmed and sliced
450–500g cooked chicken, shredded
    (i.e. 1 x 1.6kg chicken, roasted, see page 113)
100g cooked ham, fat discarded and
    cut into thin strips

To make the pastry, rub the butter into the flour with a little salt, then add the whole egg and bring the dough together with a drop of water (you can also make it in a food processor). Wrap it in clingfilm and chill for at least 1 hour. It can be made a day or two in advance.

To make the filling, melt 50g of the butter in a medium, non-stick saucepan over a medium heat, stir in the flour and let the roux seethe for a moment. Then, working off the heat, gradually stir in the stock and crème fraîche. Bring the sauce to the boil, then simmer over a low heat for 10 minutes, stirring occasionally. Season with salt and pepper and stir in the mustard and tarragon.

In the meantime, cook the mushrooms – you will need to do this in two batches. Heat half the remaining butter and 1 tablespoon of the olive oil in a large frying pan over a high heat. Add half the shallots and garlic and stir for a moment until sizzling, then add half the mushrooms, season and fry them for a few minutes until lightly coloured. Transfer to a bowl and cook the remainder likewise. Stir the mushroom mixture, chicken and ham into the sauce and set it aside to cool.

Heat the oven to 210°C (190°C fan oven) gas mark 7. Thinly roll out two-thirds of the pastry on a lightly floured surface and line a deep 1.5–1.7 litre pie dish. Trim any excess pastry hanging over the sides and fill the pastry case with the chicken and mushroom filling. Roll out the remaining pastry, including the trimmings, paint the rim just above the filling with the eggwash and lay the lid in place. Trim it, leaving 1cm for shrinkage. Press the edges together and, using your fingers, press into scallops. Brush the top with the eggwash and cut out some leaves from the trimmings. Using the tip of a sharp knife, trace veins on the leaves, then place them in the centre or around the outside of the pie, and paint with eggwash.

Bake the pie for 45–50 minutes, by which time both the pastry on the top and that lining the dish should be nice and golden. Serve the pie straight away.

You can also make the pie a day in advance and chill it, in which case chill the filling before assembling it and decorate with the leaves, securing them with a little eggwash, but save glazing the surface until just before you pop the pie into the oven. It might need a few minutes' longer cooking.

Roasting your chicken

If you keep it simple enough, there's every reason for popping a chicken into the oven any day of the week. A salt and pepper bird is just that: a sprinkling of sea salt and grinding of black pepper; there is enough fat beneath the skin to baste it. Only a little more elaborate – coat a 1.6kg free-range chicken with olive oil and season it; pop some thyme, a smashed garlic clove or two and half an onion into the cavity and roast for 50–55 minutes at 220°C (200°C fan oven) gas mark 7 until the skin is golden and the juices run clear.

I have always liked the raw honesty of Victorian pub advertisements: 'GIN – drunk for a penny, dead drunk for two', which reflects the state of this guinea fowl before it hits the pot, having been steeped in a bath of red wine and brandy that infuses its already dark and rich flesh.

Guinea fowl don't come in anything as convenient as a size to feed six – the average available bird weighs in at about 1.2kg – so when quartered it will do for four. When making this recipe, I would order a couple of birds and freeze the remaining two quarters for another time. It can, of course, also be made with a large chicken, upwards of 1.7kg, in which case this can be jointed into eight or ten. I rather like having a small piece of meat and going back for more.

If you fancy a more Mediterranean feel, you could leave out the cloves and add 180g rinsed and pitted Kalamata olives halfway through. I would serve the casserole with buttered spinach and boiled potatoes with lashings of salty butter.

Drunken guinea fowl

Serves 6

½ bottle red wine

2 tbsp brandy

2 tsp thyme leaves

1 bay leaf, broken into pieces

3 garlic cloves, peeled and crushed to a paste

1½ x 1.2kg guinea fowl, quartered

1kg beefsteak tomatoes

extra virgin olive oil

6 shallots, peeled, halved and sliced

sea salt and black pepper

2 cloves

a pinch of dried chilli flakes

First marinate the guinea fowl, either overnight or for an hour or two in the morning. Combine the wine, brandy, thyme, bay leaf and garlic in a large bowl, add the jointed guinea fowl and coat it in the marinade, then cover and chill, turning the pieces and basting halfway through.

Bring a medium pan of water to the boil. Cut out a small cone from the top of each tomato to remove the core, plunge them into the boiling water for 20 seconds (you may need to do this in batches) and then into cold water. Slip off the skins and coarsely chop the flesh.

Heat 3 tablespoons of olive oil in a large casserole over a medium heat, add the shallots and fry for a few minutes, stirring occasionally until lightly coloured, then add the tomatoes and cook for about 15 minutes, pressing them down occasionally, until you have a thick purée.

At the same time, heat 1 tablespoon of olive oil in a large frying pan over a highish heat. Pat the guinea fowl dry on a double thickness of kitchen paper, season and then sear to colour on both sides. You will need to do this in two goes. Working off the heat, pour the marinade into the frying pan and stir to take up the sticky residue on the bottom of the pan. Stir the marinade into the tomato base, add the cloves, chilli and season, then add the guinea fowl and press to submerge it as far as possible. Bring to the boil, then cover the pan and cook over a low heat for 1 hour.

Transfer the guinea fowl pieces to a large bowl and cover to keep warm. Simmer the juices over a high heat until reduced by about a third and really rich to taste. At this point you can hunt around for the cloves and discard them. Return the guinea fowl to the pan and serve.

I first discovered the joys of slow-roasting duck when I miscalculated the cooking time one New Year's Eve, and there was no way of bringing dinner forward without ruining the rhythm of the evening. Everyone would have been fast asleep in front of the fire by the time midnight struck. So I turned the oven down and hoped for the best, and it was quite superb. I now have to steel myself to cook duck in any other way. And in case you are worried that this might mean succulent meat at the cost of a crisp skin, fear not – by whacking the temperature up at the very end to colour and crisp the outside, you can have the best of both worlds.

Take advantage, too, of the copious fat given off by the duck to sauté some potatoes to accompany it. I prefer not to prick the duck's skin because the fat bastes the flesh as it cooks, and any excess finds a way out into the roasting dish in due course.

Waxy potatoes cooked with the skin on ensure lots of crispy splinters to pick at – Charlotte, Pink Fir Apple and La Ratte are all contenders.

Roast duck with sauté potatoes

Serves 4

For the duck

1 x 2.2–2.5kg oven-ready duck (farmed duck is
    preferable to wild in this case)
sea salt
a handful each of sage leaves, rosemary and
    thyme sprigs

90ml port
2 tsp plain flour
300ml giblet or chicken stock

Heat the oven to 160°C (140°C fan oven) gas mark 3. Rub the duck skin generously all over with salt, and stuff the cavity with the herbs. Place the duck breast-up (ideally on a rack) in a roasting tin and roast for 3 hours, draining the fat into a bowl at hourly intervals. Turn the oven up to 220°C (200°C fan oven) gas mark 7 and roast for another 15 minutes to colour and crisp the skin.

Transfer the duck from the rack to a board (or place it on a plate) and leave to rest for 15 minutes while you make the gravy. Skim off the fat in the roasting tray, add the port and simmer for several minutes until it is well reduced, scraping up all the sticky residue. Stir in the flour and allow to seethe briefly, then gradually blend in the stock. Bring to the boil and simmer for several minutes until rich and amalgamated, then season to taste and strain into a warm jug or gravy boat.

Carve the duck, or pull it apart, making sure you get all of the skin, which should be oily and crisp top and bottom. Serve with the gravy and sauté potatoes.

Sauté potatoes

600g salad or waxy potatoes, scrubbed
3 tbsp rendered duck fat
10 unpeeled garlic cloves

sea salt and black pepper
a handful of sage leaves

While the duck is roasting, bring a large pan of salted water to the boil, add the potatoes, bring back to the boil and cook for 15–25 minutes until tender. Drain into a colander and leave to cool.

Half an hour before eating, slice the potatoes. Heat the fat in a frying pan over a low heat and sauté the potatoes and garlic for 20–25 minutes. Season and keep turning until crisp. Add the sage 10 minutes before the end. Serve when ready.

5
Fish

Since I find the world of rubs, pastes, marinades and mops to be a dark art, all too often an excuse to throw together any mismatched combination of spices and herbs, this marinade is simplicity itself. I like to be able to read through a list of ingredients and conjour in my mind the end taste.

The smell of prawn shells toasting over hot coals on a warm, breezy day is one of the most appetising I know. It sets in motion a chain reaction of thinking ... grilled prawns, Bloody Mary, hammock.

Prawn brochettes

Makes 6 x 20cm skewers

24 raw, unshelled large prawns (300–500g)

For the marinade
1 tsp fennel seeds

1 tbsp lemon juice
2 tbsp extra virgin olive oil
1 tsp finely chopped medium-hot red chilli

Grind the fennel seeds in a pestle and mortar, then combine with the rest of the ingredients for the marinade. Add the prawns, stir to coat, then cover and chill for about 45 minutes. Meanwhile, if you are using wooden skewers, put them in cold water to soak.

Thread the prawns onto the skewers. Just before grilling, baste with the marinade and season with salt.

Outdoors: Cook for 1–2 minutes on each side.
Indoors: Place a ridged griddle over a medium-high heat and cook for 1–2 minutes on each side.

I have had a soft spot for mackerel with its glossy, blue-black skin ever since reeling them in from a small fishing boat in Salcombe's bay as a child. Every time you lowered a baited hook, so too a mackerel bit within minutes. It was enormously satisfying, and we caught so many that I wasn't in the least suspicious many years later, holidaying on the coast of Ireland, when my husband and a friend arrived back at the house to a hero's welcome with a box of mackerel after a day's fishing in the pouring rain. They had, of course, spent the day in the pub, and bought the fish on the quayside. The box should have given it away, but I guess we were just very glad of supper.

Partly in response to its detractors, I am always on the lookout for ways to serve this fish that might convert the sceptical. More recently I've been enjoying it as 'escabèche', grilled and steeped in a sweet and sour marinade with carrots, onions, bay leaves and saffron. Not so much pickled as lightly soused, the fish taste even better the next day.

Mackerel escabèche

Serves 4 (main course) or 8 (starter)

2 good-sized mackerel (about 500g each), or
    4 small fish, filleted
olive oil for brushing
sea salt and black pepper

For the marinade
4 tbsp extra virgin olive oil
100ml water
1 tsp sea salt

100ml dry white wine
1 tbsp white wine vinegar
2 slim carrots, trimmed, peeled and finely sliced
    into rings
2 bay leaves
3 garlic cloves, peeled and smashed
a pinch of saffron filaments (about 20)
a pinch of chilli flakes
½ tsp caster sugar

To make the marinade, place 2 tablespoons of the olive oil, the water and salt in a small saucepan with the rest of the marinade ingredients. Put the remaining olive oil to one side. Bring the marinade ingredients to the boil, then simmer for about 20 minutes (making sure the vegetables are submerged), until the vegetables are tender.

Meanwhile, place a ridged griddle (ideally non-stick) over a medium-high heat. Using a very sharp knife, score the mackerel skin diagonally at 2cm intervals, brush with olive oil and season on both sides. Grill for 1–2 minutes (depending on their size) on the skin side, then turn and grill the flesh side for 1–2 minutes, leaving them slightly underdone in the centre.

Arrange the fish skin-side up in a shallow dish. Stir the reserved olive oil into the hot marinade and pour it over the fish. Leave to cool completely (about 2 hours). They can also be made up to a day in advance: cover and chill them, and bring back to room temperature 30 minutes before eating.

While we may be most familiar with salmon as a poached fish, poaching is a delightful way of cooking any number of other fish, though for some reason it is a method that seems to have been all but lost to time. On trawling the internet it becomes a little clearer, when entry after entry links poaching to dieting. And while it's good to know that it's suitably healthy, there are better reasons for turning to it more often.

You want nice thick skate wings with juicy skeins of white flesh for this elegant salad. Small ones tend to collapse when you flake them. Ideally, ask your fishmonger to skin the skate, but don't worry if he doesn't – it can easily be removed after poaching. As always with fish, freshness is everything.

Skate and potato salad tartare

Serves 4

2 carrots, peeled and thickly sliced
2 sticks of celery, trimmed and halved
2 bay leaves
150ml dry vermouth or white wine
1.2 litres water
1 tsp sea salt
a pinch of black pepper
1kg skate wings, skinned
600g medium-sized new potatoes, scrubbed or
　　peeled as necessary
1 spring onion, trimmed and finely sliced

For the dressing
200ml sour cream
½ tsp Dijon mustard
sea salt
2 tbsp small capers, rinsed
1 tbsp gherkins, finely chopped
2 tbsp finely chopped flat-leaf parsley

Place the carrots, celery and bay leaves in a large, cast-iron casserole with the vermouth or wine, the water, salt and a little black pepper. Bring the liquid to the boil, then cover the pan and simmer over a low heat for 15 minutes.

Submerge the skate wings in the liquid, cover and poach gently for 10–15 minutes depending on thickness; the flesh should come away from the bone with ease. Transfer to a plate and leave to cool.

Add the potatoes to the pan and bring to the boil, then cook for 15–20 minutes until tender. Drain into a colander and leave to cool.

To make the dressing, blend the sour cream, mustard and a little salt in a bowl. Set aside half the capers and stir the remainder into the sour cream together with the gherkins and parsley.

Carefully scrape any membrane off the surface of the skate flesh, remove the flesh from the cartilage and separate it into strips. You can prepare the salad to this point in advance, in which case cover the potatoes and fish, set them aside and chill the dressing.

To serve, slice the potatoes, arrange them on four plates, season and scatter the skate on top. Drizzle over the dressing and sprinkle over the reserved whole capers and the spring onion.

Eating crabs has everything to do with culture, something that isn't lost on the French and Spanish. Sitting round a table in the dim light of a candle as the assembled company goes to work with a hammer, a pair of nutcrackers and a pick has a delicious sense of ritual. With the anticipation of every sweet and hard-won morsel, the process itself is central to the occasion and demands that we linger and take our time. It is the same pleasure as working your way from the outside of an artichoke to its heart, prising open mussels to extract the meat within, or scooping the flesh of an oyster clean off its shell with a morsel of bread.

Eating crab with mayonnaise, in my book, surpasses any other way of enjoying it. This recipe may give you more crabmeat than you need per person, but I don't see much point in going at anything smaller. And the crabmeat is unlikely to go to waste. Aside from a fresh crab sandwich, potted crab takes all of ten minutes to prepare and is a rare treat.

A spoonful of mustard not only stabilises the mayonnaise but also adds a welcome savour. Groundnut oil ensures the emulsion is creamy and light in texture – the use of extra virgin olive oil would overwhelm the crab, and garlic would be a heresy.

Crab with mayonnaise

Serves 4

For the crab
4 x 1kg cooked crabs
crusty white bread, to serve

The white crabmeat is to be found in three places: the claws (which give most generously), the spindly legs, and the cavities within the body; the brown meat, which is sometimes almost wet and at other times quite dry, mainly lines the upper shell. First arm yourself with the necessary arsenal of equipment – a large bowl for the debris, a breadboard, a rolling pin, a mallet or hammer, and a pair of nutcrackers (nothing too fancy here like a squirrel whose jaws pose as a tool, but a straightforward pair shaped like pliers).

Remove the claw and three legs beside it, on either side, by breaking them off where they are attached to the body. Using the end of the rolling pin on a board, smash all three joints of the claws. As crabs get larger the shells of their claws can get really tough, so you may need to be pretty forceful. Picking off the broken shell, extract the crabmeat.

Now, using the nutcracker, crack the joints of the legs and carefully pick out the meat inside. You will need to employ a crabpick or skewer here to extract every last bit. To my taste this is that much sweeter and finer in texture than the claw meat.

And now for the messy bit. Insert a sharp knife between the upper shell and the body at the opposite end to the tail and lever the body section loose. Lift it free of the shell and pull it off. There will be a little brown meat clinging to the underside. Spoon this out, then cut the body in half. You may find some more brown meat inside. Using a skewer, pick out the white meat from the row of cavities in each half.

Now scrape out the brown meat lining the upper shell with a teaspoon. Pick the crabmeat over for any stray splinters, et voilà! You may have savoured the crabmeat along the way, otherwise you will by now have a lovely big pile of succulent white and creamy brown meat to enjoy with mayonnaise (below) and crusty bread.

Mayonnaise

Serves 4

1 medium egg yolk at room temperature
1 tsp Dijon mustard
a pinch of fine sea salt

about 220ml groundnut oil
a squeeze of lemon juice

Place the egg yolk in a bowl with the mustard and salt and whisk to blend them. Now add just a dribble of oil and whisk it in, then another and another until you can see the sauce thickening and you are confident that the mayonnaise is taking.

You can now start to add the oil in bolder streams, whisking with each addition. By the end, the mayonnaise should be so thick that it clings to the whisk and sits in mounds in the bowl. Add a squeeze of lemon juice, cover and chill until required.

I recall, when holidaying in the Hebrides, hanging around in anticipation as the fishing boats docked. The fishermen would descend with a large bag of claws in hand that they were only too happy to give away. Presumably their wives had long tired of the gift. Again, claws are a common sight on the Continent, but here dressed or frozen crab is more likely the norm, and I cannot be doing with the latter, which has the texture of cotton wool and is watery to boot. But dressed fresh crab is a fine enough convenience. Richly flavoured and textured, these are more luxurious than your normal fishcake.

Maryland crabcakes

Serves 4 (main course) or 6 (starter)

For the crabcakes
50g water biscuits or cream crackers
1 medium egg, beaten
2 tbsp mayonnaise
2 tsp Dijon mustard
a shake of Lea and Perrins
1 tbsp lemon juice
sea salt and black pepper
450g white and brown crabmeat,
    picked over (see page 126)

4 tbsp coarsely chopped flat-leaf parsley
1 tbsp groundnut oil

For the relish
6 spring onions, trimmed and finely sliced
2 tbsp capers, rinsed
1 tbsp lemon juice
4 tbsp groundnut oil

First reduce the biscuits or crackers to fine crumbs, either by placing them inside a plastic bag and crushing them using a rolling pin, or by whizzing them in a food processor. Whisk the egg with the mayonnaise, mustard, Lea and Perrins, lemon juice and a little seasoning in a bowl. Blend this with the crabmeat, then stir in the cracker crumbs. Cover and set aside in a cool place for 30 minutes for the crackers to absorb any moisture and the mixture to firm up, then stir in the parsley.

Taking a tablespoon of mixture at a time, shape 12 flattened crabcakes and place on a couple of large plates.

Combine all the ingredients for the relish in a small bowl with a pinch of salt.

To cook all the crabcakes at once you will need to have two frying pans on the go. Otherwise, cook them in two batches, and keep the first batch warm in a low oven while you cook the second. In this case there shouldn't be any need to add more oil to the pan after the first batch. Heat the groundnut oil in a large frying pan over a medium heat and cook the crabcakes for 3 minutes on each side, turning with a palette knife, until lightly golden. Drain them on a double thickness of kitchen paper, then serve with the relish.

These rustic fishcakes are delectably crisp underneath, and the rasher of streaky bacon that runs around them works a treat with the haddock. Being baked rather than fried makes them a star dish for entertaining – you could serve one as a starter, or a couple as a main course.

Oven-baked, smoked haddock fishcakes

Serves 6

For the fishcakes
600g maincrop potatoes, peeled and halved or
    quartered if large
500g undyed smoked haddock fillets
350ml full-cream milk
1 bay leaf
sea salt and black pepper
1 medium egg
12 unsmoked streaky bacon rashers
groundnut or vegetable oil for roasting

For the sauce
30g unsalted butter
25g plain flour
150ml double cream
½ tsp mild curry powder
1 tsp tomato purée
a generous squeeze of lemon juice
a few drops of Tabasco

You may have cooked your potatoes in advance; if not, cook as described on page 125. At the same time, arrange the haddock fillets in a pan in a single layer, pour over the milk, tuck in the bay leaf and season with black pepper. Bring the milk to the boil, then almost cover the pan with a lid, leaving a gap for the steam to escape, and cook over a low heat for 5 minutes. Transfer the haddock fillets to a plate and leave for 10 minutes.

Drain the potatoes into a sieve, leave for a few minutes for the surface water to evaporate, then mash them coarsely. Add any juices from the resting fish to the haddock milk. Flake the haddock, discarding skin and bones, add it to the potato and blend. Taste the mixture for seasoning, then add the egg and blend once more.

Take heaped tablespoons of the mixture and form into 12 fishcakes. Set these aside on a couple of plates or on a tray. Loosely wrap a bacon rasher around each fishcake, with the ends underneath, bearing in mind that the bacon will shrink as it cooks. You can prepare the fishcakes to this point a day or two in advance.

To make the sauce, melt the butter in a small, non-stick saucepan, stir in the flour and cook the roux for about a minute until it is seething and floury. Working off the heat, gradually blend in the haddock milk and then stir in the cream, curry powder and tomato purée. Bring the sauce to the boil, stirring constantly, then cook over a low heat for 10 minutes. Season with salt, a generous squeeze of lemon and a dash of Tabasco.

Heat the oven to 220°C (200°C fan oven) gas mark 7. Arrange the fishcakes on a roasting tray, drizzle over some oil and bake for 30 minutes until they are golden and crisp, basting them halfway through. Reheat the sauce if necessary and serve spooned over the fishcakes.

Sardines, brown bread, olive oil and a mass of green leafy herbs sounds like a cardiologist's dream, so it is especially satisfying that this recipe is basically fish and chips. Serve with a simple tomato salad – different varieties, roughly hewn, seasoned with salt and sugar, doused in olive oil and scattered with slivers of spring onion.

If you are increasing the quantity you will need to use bigger trays to ensure both chips and sardines colour and crisp evenly. You could, in this instance, roast the potatoes, and keep these warm while you pop the sardines in to cook. In the absence of the salsa verde, use a scattering of chopped parsley and some lemon wedges.

If you can find the time to chop all the ingredients for the salsa verde finely by hand. you will be well rewarded. Otherwise, chop the herbs, garlic and capers in a food processor, then remove them and stir in the anchovies, olive oil, lemon juice and mustard.

Crispy sardines with oven-roasted chips and salsa verde

Serves 4 (main course) or 6 (starter)

For the fish
100g fresh brown breadcrumbs
  (see page 62)
6 sardines, filleted
4 tbsp extra virgin olive oil
plain flour
1 egg, beaten

For the chips
1.2kg large waxy potatoes, peeled
finely grated zest of 1 lemon, plus 1 tbsp
  lemon juice
2 tbsp extra virgin olive oil
40g unsalted butter
sea salt and black pepper

Heat the oven to 220°C (200°C fan oven) gas mark 7. Spread the breadcrumbs in a thin layer on two baking trays and toast them for 6–8 minutes until lightly golden. Remove and leave to cool.

For the chips, slice the potatoes lengthways into pieces 1cm thick, then cut these into thick chips. Arrange in a roasting dish (about 38cm x 25cm) with the lemon zest. Drizzle over the olive oil and lemon juice, dot with the butter and season. Cover with foil and roast for 20 minutes.

Loosen the chips with a spatula, give them a stir and roast uncovered for another 30–35 minutes until deliciously golden and caramelised, stirring again halfway through.

Towards the end of cooking the chips, pat the sardine fillets dry with kitchen paper. Scrunch the breadcrumbs between your fingers to break up any clumps and toss them in a shallow bowl with some seasoning and the olive oil until evenly and lightly coated. Have the flour and egg at the ready in another couple of shallow bowls.

Coat the sardine fillets with the flour. Dip into the egg and then into the breadcrumbs, and arrange on a roasting tray, spaced slightly apart. Bake for 6–8 minutes until crisp and lightly golden. Serve the sardines and chips straight away, with the salsa verde.

Salsa verde

3 heaped tbsp finely chopped basil
2 heaped tbsp finely chopped mint
6 heaped tbsp finely chopped flat-leaf parsley
½ garlic clove, peeled and finely chopped
6 salted anchovies, finely chopped

2 tbsp capers, rinsed and finely chopped
6 tbsp extra virgin olive oil
a squeeze of lemon juice
1 tsp Dijon mustard

Combine the herbs, garlic, anchovies and capers in a bowl, then stir in the olive oil, lemon juice and mustard.

This stew has everything to do with sopping up bisque-scented juices – the morsels of langoustine are an added bonus. Langoustines are always a treat, but any large, uncooked and unshelled prawns will do. Allow about six per person, bearing in mind that the cooking time may vary. I never see fennel herb for sale, but it grows profusely in my garden and self-seeds with abandon, and you too may have some close to hand.

Langoustine stew

Serves 4

extra virgin olive oil

4 shallots, peeled, halved and sliced

2 sticks of celery, trimmed and sliced

1 carrot, peeled, halved and sliced

3 garlic cloves, peeled and finely chopped

500ml fresh tomato sauce (see page 170)

black pepper

1kg langoustines

finely chopped fennel, dill or parsley

crusty bread, to serve

Heat a couple of tablespoons of olive oil in a large cast-iron casserole over a medium heat. Add the shallots, celery and carrot and sweat for 10–15 minutes until lightly coloured, adding the garlic towards the end and stirring now and again. Add the tomato sauce, season with black pepper and bring to a simmer.

At the same time, bring a large pan of heavily salted water to the boil, add the langoustines and cook for 3 minutes, then drain into a sieve. Add them to the sauce, stir, cover and cook over a medium heat for about 5 minutes.

Serve in shallow bowls with a splash of olive oil, chopped fennel, dill or parsley, and plenty of bread on the side.

Trout is a fish we could make more of, but like salmon, there are vast differentials between well and poorly farmed fish. Organic trout farming is a comparatively recent departure, but in terms of quality it is where the future lies (see Suppliers, page 202).

Truite au bleu is a fisherman's sleight of hand, also beloved of restaurants with a trout pond or a tank containing the live fish. Beyond being fresh, the fish must actually be alive. Just before being delivered to the pot, they are stunned and gutted. It is the slime coating the fish – which we try so assiduously to wash off – that explains the name of the dish, as it turns a ghostly shade of blue in contact with vinegar. This softens the skin in the process, though I feel only the hardy would be tempted to eat it. Even without the newly landed slime and blue of the skin, this is still an excellent method for cooking whole trout.

Dill is particularly good with fish and with cucumber, but not always easy to track down. If you can't get hold of any, chives would be the next best herb.

Poached trout with yogurt, cucumber and dill sauce

Serves 4

For the poached trout

2 carrots, trimmed, peeled and sliced

2 sticks of celery, trimmed and sliced

1 onion, peeled and chopped

1 bay leaf

a few parsley stalks

500ml dry white wine

500ml water

4 x 250g trout, cleaned

150ml white wine vinegar

30g coarse sea salt

chopped dill, to serve

You will need to start preparing the trout several hours in advance of eating. Place the vegetables and herbs in a medium saucepan with the wine and water. Bring to the boil, then cover the pan and simmer over a low heat for 30 minutes.

Towards the end of this time, arrange the fish top to tail on their sides in a 30cm oval casserole. Bring the vinegar to the boil in a small saucepan with the salt, stirring until it dissolves, and pour evenly over the fish – any slime coating them should turn a greyish blue. Pour the hot court-bouillon over the fish, bring it back to a healthy boil over a medium-high heat, then cover and leave for several hours to cool, until tepid.

Carefully lift the fish out of the court-bouillon onto plates to serve, dabbing any liquid that seeps out with kitchen paper. Accompany with the yogurt, cucumber and dill sauce, scattering over a little chopped dill.

Yogurt, cucumber and dill sauce

2tbsp extra virgin olive oil
4 shallots, peeled and finely chopped
1 cucumber, peeled, quartered, deseeded and
    diced
sea salt and black pepper

4 tbsp chopped dill
½ tsp caster sugar
300g Greek yogurt
a squeeze of lemon juice

Heat the olive oil in a large frying pan over a medium heat and sweat the shallots for a minute or two, stirring occasionally until softened, without colouring. Add the cucumber, season and sweat for a few minutes, stirring now and then. Transfer the vegetables to a bowl, stir in the dill and sugar and leave to cool. You can prepare the sauce to this point a couple of hours in advance.

Shortly before serving, stir in the Greek yogurt and a squeeze of lemon juice.

There is a certain decade of life, normally your twenties, when poached salmon becomes a regular feature, following in the wake of every wedding you are invited to. So much so that, like roast turkey at Christmas, you develop a love-hate relationship with it – on the one hand comforted by the sense of ritual, familiarity and sheer Englishness, and on the other cursing its dry, tough, pink flesh. Because, like a roast turkey, while it can be sublime, it can also be a disappointment.

But however hackneyed, poaching salmon is one of the finest fates for this fish, and with a little care its rich, oily flesh is rendered supremely succulent and moist.

Years ago, through necessity, I learnt how to poach a salmon without a fish kettle, and to this day I don't possess one. It joins a long list of specialised equipment that only clutter up the cupboard, when an all-round item of kitchen equipment will do the job just as well. To this end, a preserving pan is a must. As well as doing for chutney and marmalade, it makes a great stockpot, copes with boiling potatoes for the masses and poaching a salmon whole. Although, instead of poaching the fish lengthways, the salmon is coiled and lain within a tea towel that then acts as a sling to lift it out, which does away with the need for a removable rack. The fish remains coiled once it is cooked – no bad thing given that most of us have more large circular plates than long ones.

A salmon weighing 1.8kg is considered small, but is the ideal size for six or eight people, and the flesh of a small fish is more delicate. If farmed, this size fish is also less likely to be fatty. But the real seasonal treats are wild salmon and salmon trout.

Poached salmon with sorrel mayonnaise

Serves 6

For the poached salmon
1.8kg salmon, cleaned

For the poaching liquor
1 bottle dry white wine
1 carrot, peeled and sliced
2 sticks of celery, trimmed and sliced
1 leek, trimmed and sliced
3 tbsp sea salt

For the sorrel mayonnaise
1 tbsp groundnut oil
2 shallots, peeled and finely chopped
70g sorrel, stalks thickly sliced
100ml dry vermouth
150ml whipping cream
sea salt and black pepper
1 quantity Mayonnaise (see page 127)

First make the sorrel mayonnaise. Heat the groundnut oil in a small saucepan over a medium heat, add the shallots and sweat them for a few minutes until they soften and turn translucent. Add the sorrel and stir until it changes colour, then pour in the vermouth and simmer until well reduced and the sorrel is sitting in a buttery emulsion. Pour in the cream, add some seasoning and bring to the boil, then simmer until reduced by half. Tip the contents of the pan into a liquidiser or food processor and purée. Transfer to a bowl, cover with clingfilm and leave to cool.

Fold the sorrel cream into the mayonnaise, cover and chill until required. It should keep well for several days.

Place all the ingredients for the poaching liquor in a large saucepan. Measure the maximum height of the fish and add water to the pan to this level, in order to fully immerse the fish when you add it later. Cover the pan and bring to a rolling boil.

Place the salmon on top of a clean tea towel in an upright position, curved to fit the pot. (Remove the salmon head if you prefer.) Pin the corners with a safety pin. Lower the salmon into the boiling liquid, bring back to the boil, then cover the pan with a lid, remove from the heat and leave for several hours to cool. The salmon will be at its best if removed when the water is at blood temperature; you can leave it overnight, but this will make it a tiny bit overcooked to my taste.

Once the fish is ready, lift it onto a plate, undo the pins and carefully slip the tea towel from underneath it. Drain off any liquid that collects in the bottom of the plate. Using a knife, lift off the skin and remove the fatty core running down the spine. Loosen the salmon flesh from the spine in large fillets and place them on cold plates, picking out any visible bones. Serve the sorrel mayonnaise dolloped on top.

A fish pie is an essential part of a country repertoire, and I've been making this one for years – cider, mustard, capers and crème fraîche underpin its character, while the milk from poaching the haddock forms the basis of the sauce that binds the fish. This gives it a head start over a plain béchamel. The idea is to have a selection of fish, with contrasting textures and flavours, and, as ever, to be guided by what's on offer seasonally.

Fish pie with capers

Serves 6

800g haddock fillets (skin on), or other flaky
    white fish
250ml full-cream milk
1 bay leaf
sea salt and black pepper
250g scallops
200g shelled raw prawns
1 tbsp small salted capers, rinsed

For the béchamel
60g unsalted butter
50g plain flour

150ml dry cider
150g crème fraîche
1 heaped tsp Dijon mustard

For the mash
1.5kg maincrop potatoes, peeled and halved, or
    quartered if large
100g crème fraîche
50g unsalted butter
2 large egg yolks

Place the fish in a large saucepan. Pour over the milk, tuck in the bay leaf, season and bring to the boil. Cover with a lid, leaving a gap for steam to escape, and cook on a low heat for 4 minutes. Strain the cooking liquid into a bowl. Once the fish is cool enough to handle, flake it as coarsely as possible, discarding the skin. If any additional liquid is given out at this point, discard it.

Pull off the white gristle at the side of each scallop, removing the surrounding girdle, then cut off and reserve the coral and slice each scallop into 2 or 3 discs.

To make the béchamel, melt the butter in a medium, non-stick saucepan, stir in the flour and allow the roux to seethe for a minute. Working off the heat, very gradually work in the cider and the fish cooking liquor, then the crème fraîche and the mustard. Bring to the boil, stirring constantly, and simmer over a very low heat for 5–10 minutes, stirring occasionally. If any butter separates out, simply stir vigorously until it is reincorporated.

Taste to check the seasoning, then fold in the haddock, scallops, prawns and capers. Transfer the fish to a 35cm oval gratin dish or other ovenproof dish with a 2.5 litre capacity that offers a large surface area to crisp. Cover the surface with clingfilm and leave the fish to cool, which will help prevent the potato from sinking in when you spoon it on top.

Bring a large pan of salted water to the boil, add the potatoes and cook until they are tender. Drain them into a sieve or colander and leave for a few minutes for the surface moisture to evaporate. Pass through a mouli-légumes or a sieve back into the pan. Heat the crème fraîche with the butter and some seasoning and beat this into the mash, and then beat in the egg yolks. Smooth this over the top of the fish, forking the surface into furrows. At this stage, you can cover and chill the pie until required, for up to 48 hours.

When ready to cook, heat the oven to 200°C (180°C fan oven) gas mark 6 and bake the pie for 35–40 minutes until crusty and golden on the surface. If cooking from chilled, it may need a little longer in the oven.

6

Vegetables

The distinguishing feature of a Russian salad, which has come to mean almost any combination of cold, diced vegetables dressed with mayonnaise (though potato is de rigueur), is the sharpening touch of some capers, gherkins, pickled walnuts, or anchovies. Sometimes diced chicken and seafood are added. Here the bits on the side turn it into a slightly more lavish spread than the salad on its own, which can accompany all manner of cold cuts.

Russian salad

Serves 4

For the salad

100g fine French beans, topped and tailed and
 cut into 1cm dice
100g sugar snaps, topped and tailed and cut into
 1cm dice
200g peas, fresh or frozen
400g cooked waxy potatoes, cut into 1cm dice
2 tbsp small capers, rinsed
2 tsp finely chopped tarragon or 2 tbsp chopped
 chervil
2 spring onions, trimmed and finely sliced

For the mayonnaise

1 medium egg yolk, at room temperature
1 tsp Dijon mustard
sea salt
about 220ml groundnut or other vegetable oil
2 tsp red or white wine vinegar

To serve

12 quail's eggs
12 shell-on, cooked langoustines or tiger prawns
inner celery heart, trimmed, or small romaine
 lettuce leaves

Bring a medium pan of water to the boil, add the French beans and simmer for 1 minute, then add the sugar snaps and fresh peas and cook for a further 2 minutes. They should be just tender by the end. If using frozen peas, cook them separately to avoid losing the boiling point. Drain the vegetables and refresh under the cold tap, then leave to cool completely.

To make the mayonnaise, place the egg yolk in a bowl with the mustard and a pinch of salt and whisk to blend. Now, add just a dribble of oil and whisk it in, then another and another until you can see the sauce thickening and you are confident that the mayonnaise is taking. You can now start to add the oil in bolder streams, whisking with each addition. By the end the mayonnaise should be so thick that it clings to the whisk and sits in mounds in the bowl. Stir in the vinegar.

To assemble the salad, combine the potato, green vegetables, capers, tarragon or chervil, the spring onions and mayonnaise in a bowl, then transfer to a serving dish.

For the quail's eggs, bring a small pan of water to the boil, add the eggs and simmer them for 2½ minutes (sorry to be so precise, but there is a big difference between two and three minutes). Run cold water into the pan and once it is cool, remove the eggs to a bowl.

Serve the Russian salad with the quail's eggs, langoustines or prawns, and celery heart or romaine leaves.

The recent arrival of 'Continental' spring onions, for which read 'popular in France', is to be welcomed. Fatter and juicier than the diminutive drainpipes usually found bundled with a rubber band, they lend themselves to being sliced wafer thin and scattered over all manner of salads. I have a particular soft spot for the purple ones, a colour that is skin-deep, giving way to pearly white rings within.

This is one of the prettiest salads I know, and the most delicious. Pomegranates it has to be – no other fruit can charm a bowl of green leaves with quite the same pizzazz.

Spinach, spring onion and pomegranate salad

Serves 4

a mixture of young spinach leaves and wild
   rocket to feed four
1 pomegranate
extra virgin olive oil

lemon juice
sea salt
4 spring onions, trimmed and finely sliced
   diagonally

Wash the salad leaves in cold water, then spin them in a salad spinner or place them in a clean tea towel, gather up the corners and give it a jolly good shake. Place the leaves in a bowl.

Halve the pomegranate and, pressing down on the skin of each half, pop the seeds out into a bowl. Pick out any white membranes and discard the juice.

To serve the salad, drizzle over a little olive oil and, using your hands, gently toss to coat the leaves. Now squeeze over a little lemon juice, scrunch over a few crystals of sea salt, scatter over half the spring onion slices and toss. Scatter over the remaining spring onion and the pomegranate seeds and serve.

Perfect alfresco fare, be it a picnic or lazy summer lunch in the garden. This is one of those exuberant salads that tempts you from a deli counter in its white china dish, and is good-natured enough to sit around for a couple of hours.

Should you produce some goat's cheese, any vegetarians in the party should be more than happy, too. You could also use tenderstem broccoli.

Salad of grilled broccoli, dates and almonds

Serves 6

2 red onions, peeled, halved and sliced
extra virgin olive oil
75g flaked almonds
600g purple-sprouting broccoli
sea salt and black pepper
100g dates, stoned and cut into thin strips

For the dressing
2 tbsp lemon juice
1 garlic clove, peeled and crushed to a paste
4 tbsp olive oil

Heat the oven to 200°C (180°C fan oven) gas mark 6. Toss the onions in a bowl with 1 tablespoon of olive oil, separating out the strands. Scatter them over a baking tray and roast for 15–20 minutes until golden, giving them a stir halfway through, then remove and leave to cool.

At the same time, spread the almonds in a thin layer over the base of a baking dish and toast for 10–12 minutes until golden, then remove and leave to cool.

Bring a large pan of salted water to the boil. Trim the broccoli stalks, and if they are as thick as a finger, slit them in half lengthways to ensure that the flowers cook at the same rate. Add these to the pan, cover and cook for 4 minutes, then drain into a colander and leave to cool.

Heat a ridged griddle over a medium heat, brush one side of the broccoli with olive oil, season and grill this side for 1–2 minutes until lightly golden. Brush the top side, turn and grill for another 1–2 minutes, then transfer it to a serving plate or bowl. You will need to cook it in batches. Toss the roasted onions, dates and half the flaked almonds into the broccoli.

To prepare the dressing, whisk the lemon juice with the garlic and season with a little salt, then add the olive oil. Pour over the salad and toss in the rest of the flaked almonds shortly before eating, to ensure that squeaky crisp bite.

Having always been passionate about vegetables, I find the early summer months, when the garden is raining its largesse on the kitchen, is nirvana. Everything's still young and tender, so there are peas and broad beans, French beans and sugar snaps, as well as the beginning of all the hothouse Mediterranean fare – the peppers, courgettes and aubergines that have come to define our own summertime.

But the starting point is a good stock of green vegetables. I try to cook up plenty, simply blanched in boiling, salted water and whisked out again while they're still on the crisp side. Whether they're for slipping into a green salad, dousing with olive oil and a squeeze of lemon, scattering over the top of a frittata halfway through frying, dipping into mayo, or marrying with a sliver of Parmesan, you're unlikely to regret their presence when you open the fridge door.

That little bit more exciting is to steep the cooked vegetables in olive oil with a few aromatics, some crushed garlic, chopped shallots, bruised lemon zest and perhaps some hardy herbs such as bay, thyme and rosemary. Green beans, asparagus, peas and the like actually improve with a leisurely sojourn, lapping up the flavours and oil for several days in the fridge. Though now we move on to science: it's all-important not to sharpen them with lemon juice or vinegar or to season them, until just before you eat. Anything acidic will bleach out the colour, as well as changing the flavour, and salt affects the texture of vegetables.

Marinated vegetable salad

Serves 4–6

350g shelled peas
250g mangetouts, stalk-end trimmed
250g sugar snaps, topped and tailed
2–3 garlic cloves, peeled and crushed to a paste
2 shallots, peeled and finely chopped
4 strips of lemon zest (removed with a potato peeler)
9 tbsp extra virgin olive oil

2 large handfuls of mint leaves, coarsely chopped
1 tbsp sesame seeds
2 squeezes of lemon juice, or a drop of sherry vinegar
sea salt and black pepper
150–200g ricotta
8–12 slices Parma or other air-dried ham

Bring a large pan of salted water to the boil. Add the peas and cook for 2 minutes, then add the mangetouts and sugar snaps and cook for a further 1 minute. Drain the vegetables into a colander and refresh them under the cold tap, then set aside for a few minutes for the surface moisture to evaporate.

Mix the garlic, shallots, lemon zest and olive oil in a large bowl, add the cooked vegetables and toss to coat them. Leave to cool, then mix in the mint and sesame seeds. You can eat the salad straight away or cover it and chill overnight, or longer if you wish.

Shortly before serving, discard the lemon zest, then season the salad with lemon juice or a little sherry vinegar, and salt and pepper to taste. Serve with pieces of ricotta and the Parma ham scattered on top.

I have always loved the Middle Eastern concept of eating leafy herbs as a mezze with raw vegetables and sharp cheeses, and this has inspired this otherwise Italian salad. Some black olives or strips of salted anchovies would jostle nicely in there, too.

Tomato, bread and herb salad

Serves 4

700g tomatoes (any variety will do)
sea salt
1 tsp caster sugar
150g day-old, coarse-textured white bread
   (weight excluding crusts)
extra virgin olive oil
3 tbsp water

1 small red onion, peeled, halved and finely sliced
   into half moons
black pepper
2 tsp red wine vinegar
a large handful each of basil, mint and flat-leaf
   parsley leaves

Bring a medium pan of water to the boil. Cut out a small cone from the top of each tomato to remove the core. Plunge the tomatoes into the boiling water for 20 seconds and then into cold water. Slip off the skins, quarter and cut into wedges and place in a bowl. Sprinkle over 1 teaspoon of sea salt and the sugar, and leave for 30 minutes for the juices to run.

Tear the bread into 2cm chunks and place in a bowl. Tip the tomatoes into a sieve and drain the juices into a bowl, then add 8 tablespoons of olive oil and the water. Sprinkle this on the bread and set aside for 10 minutes until is has been absorbed, stirring halfway through. The bread will take up the liquid like a sponge.

Just before serving the salad, place the tomatoes and onion in a large bowl, season with black pepper, sprinkle over the vinegar and toss. Tear the basil and mint leaves into 2 or 3 pieces and toss into the salad together with the parsley. Finally, gently mix in the bread and taste for seasoning.

Transfer the salad to a serving bowl or large plate and pour over another 4 tablespoons of olive oil.

A potato salad needn't be the ubiquitous 'in mayonnaise', but instead consist of whole new potatoes, roasted onions and cashews, and coarsely chopped leafy herbs. Most appetites can take on unlimited quantities of cold dressed potatoes, and any leftover won't go to waste – they can be sliced and sautéed or made into a tortilla a day or so later.

New potato, roasted red onion, cashew and tarragon salad

Serves 6

1.2kg small new potatoes, unpeeled, scrubbed
    if necessary
6 tbsp extra virgin olive oil
2 tbsp dry vermouth or white wine
sea salt and black pepper

4 red onions, peeled, halved and thinly sliced
2 tbsp tarragon leaves
3 tbsp snipped chives
100g roasted cashew nuts

Heat the oven to 200°C (180°C fan oven) gas mark 6 and bring a large pan of salted water to the boil. Halve any large potatoes, so they are all approximately the same size, add to the pan and boil for 20–25 minutes until tender. Drain them into a sieve and leave for a few minutes for the surface moisture to evaporate.

Transfer the potatoes to a large bowl and toss with 4 tablespoons of the olive oil, the vermouth or white wine and some seasoning, and leave until cold.

At the same time as cooking the potatoes, toss the onions in a bowl with 2 tablespoons of the oil and spread them out in a thin layer on a couple of baking sheets. Roast for 20–25 minutes until golden, giving them a stir halfway through to ensure they colour evenly. Leave to cool.

Toss the roasted onions, herbs and nuts into the potatoes and transfer to a serving bowl. The salad can be prepared a couple of hours in advance, in which case cover the bowl and set aside in a cool place.

In the heart of winter we hanker after a touch of Mediterranean sunshine in our lives. And by applying a little Italianate flair to winter vegetables – roasting them with olive oil, whole garlic cloves and woody resinous herbs – we can keep the sentiment alive throughout the cold winter months. It's not that we don't have our own tradition – parsnips cooked in the fat from the joint are a hard act to beat – but simply that the Italian approach opens wide the door to so many other types. Carrots, beetroot, squash and celeriac are just as adept at emerging crisp and singed at the fringes, and more to the point are as good for grazing on cold as hot, which must further explain why roasted veg are so central to our lives in warmer months.

As well as standing in attendance to a roast, you can leave these vegetables to cool a little and toss them into a pile of salad leaves with crispy bacon or ham, or use them, once cold, in Roasted vegetable, chestnut and barley soup (see page 49).

You want good-sized roots here – they need to be big enough to offer lovely creamy insides once they are roasted.

Roasted roots

Serves 4

4 tbsp extra virgin olive oil
4 large carrots, trimmed, peeled and quartered
    lengthways
4 large parsnips, trimmed, peeled and quartered
    lengthways

I large onion, peeled and cut into thin wedges
several bay leaves and sprigs of thyme
I head of garlic, broken into cloves
sea salt and black pepper

Heat the oven to 220°C (200°C fan oven) gas mark 7. Pour 2 tablespoons of the olive oil into a heavy-duty roasting dish on the hob over a high heat. Add the carrots and parsnips and fry for 5 minutes, stirring, then add the onion and cook for a further 5 minutes, stirring until almost coloured.

Toss in the herbs and garlic, season, pour over the remaining olive oil and roast for 30 minutes, stirring halfway through, until golden on the outside and soft within. Squeeze out the insides of the garlic cloves to eat them.

Many cold cuts could work well here, but ham marries particularly nicely with the sweetness of the vegetables.

Air-dried ham and salad of roasted roots with caper dressing

Serves 4

1 x recipe for Roasted roots
   (see page 156)
1 scant tbsp lemon juice
4 tbsp extra virgin olive oil

1 heaped tbsp capers, rinsed
2 tbsp chopped flat-leaf parsley
4 handfuls of rocket leaves
8 slices air-dried ham

Leave the roasted vegetables to cool for 10–15 minutes. To make the dressing, combine the lemon juice, olive oil, capers and parsley in a bowl.

To serve the salad, arrange the vegetables with the rocket leaves on four plates, spoon the dressing over and drape the ham alongside.

Roasting beetroot in this fashion is a great start for any salad and I've come to prefer it to boiling as a method for cooking them; the oily, roasted skins hugely enhance their charm and it's as quick and easy a method as you'll find. You will need to give the beetroot a good scrub first, of course. Serve with thick slices of a hearty country bread with a good crust.

Roasted beetroot with toasted goat's cheese

Serves 4

600g beetroot
extra virgin olive oil
3 tsp thyme leaves
sea salt and black pepper
2 tsp balsamic vinegar

1 tbsp snipped chives
1 shallot, peeled and finely chopped
2 semi-mature goat's cheeses,
    such as crottins de Chavignol

Heat the oven to 220°C (200°C fan oven) gas mark 7. Trim any beetroot stalks and roots. Pour a little olive oil into the palm of your hand, rub your hands together and then lightly coat the beetroot. Arrange them in a small baking dish, splash over a little more oil, scatter over half the thyme and season. Roast for 40 minutes, then leave to cool.

About 20 minutes before eating, heat the oven to 220°C (200°C fan oven) gas mark 7. Cut the beetroot into wedges, put on a plate and drizzle with oil and the vinegar. Then sprinkle with the chives, shallot and a little salt.

Place the goat's cheeses in a shallow ovenproof dish, scatter on the remaining thyme leaves and trickle a little oil over them. Cook for 10–12 minutes until golden and crusty at the edges. Ideally, the cheese should retain its shape while being soft and melted inside. Serve with the beetroot salad.

There are almost too many uses to name for a mixture of caramelised squash and onions, but I would suggest serving it hot with roasted partridge or quail (omitting the olives), cold with pasta shells or quills mixed in as a salad, or arranged on top of a frittata.

Roasted squash with red onion

Serves 4

2 butternut squash (about 800g each)

2 red onions, peeled, halved and cut into
  wedges

3 tbsp extra virgin olive oil,
  plus extra to serve

sea salt and black pepper

4 garlic cloves, peeled and sliced

a small handful of sage leaves

100g green and black olives, pitted

Heat the oven to 240°C (220°C fan oven) gas mark 9. Cut the skin off the squashes, quarter the bulbs to remove the seeds and slice these sections into wedges. Halve the trunks lengthways and slice into pieces 1cm thick.

Toss the squash and onions in a bowl with the olive oil and some seasoning, then arrange in a roasting dish in a crowded single layer. Roast for 20 minutes, then stir in the garlic and sage and cook for a further 20 minutes.

Leave to cool, then mix in the olives and transfer to a serving dish. Pour over a little more oil and scatter with sea salt.

I'm not sure that I've ever actually heard anyone say, 'I don't like béchamel'; they are far more likely to say, 'I don't like white sauce.' White sauce implies something that is thick, lumpy and bland, while béchamel is demurely silky with discreet hidden charms.

Its allure is that of a velvet cloak. It will elevate the most ordinary ingredients, be it cauliflower or a selection of tasty morsels destined for a pie. Of all descendants of this distinguished family, Mornay has to be the most celebrated. Care must be taken if the sauce is baked, however, when it can split or go stringy. I find the best route here is to use a couple of ounces of grated Parmesan, the feistiest cheese of all.

This recipe is a variation on the theme of cauliflower cheese, at its best eaten with a good shake of the Lea & Perrins bottle. Made with baby vegetables, it's prettier than the norm and you could include little romanescos, with their sculpted minarets, in the line-up, too – but equally you could use ordinary florets.

You can make the sauce well in advance. The vegetables can be cooked and topped with the sauce shortly before eating.

Cauliflower and broccoli gratin

Serves 4

4 mini cauliflowers, bases trimmed
4 mini broccoli, bases trimmed, or romanescos

For the béchamel
50g unsalted butter
40g plain flour

750ml full-cream milk
I bay leaf
I tsp Dijon mustard
50g freshly grated Parmesan, plus 3 tbsp
sea salt and black pepper
freshly grated nutmeg

Bring a large pan of salted water to the boil, add the cauliflowers and cook for 4–5 minutes, then add the broccoli and cook for a further 4–5 minutes until the cauliflower stalk is tender. Drain the vegetables into a colander, giving them a good shake, then leave them for a few minutes on a double thickness of kitchen paper to ensure that they are completely dry.

At the same time, make the sauce. Melt the butter in a non-stick saucepan over a medium heat, then stir in the flour and leave the roux to seethe for about a minute until it looks pale. Working off the heat, gradually beat in the milk – you should end up with a lump-free sauce the consistency of thin cream. Return the pan to the heat and bring to the boil, stirring constantly. Add the bay leaf and cook over a low heat for 5 minutes, then whisk in the mustard and the 50g Parmesan. Season with salt, pepper and nutmeg.

Heat the grill. Arrange the vegetables in a gratin dish or dishes, pour over the hot sauce, scatter with the remaining Parmesan and grill until golden and sizzling.

It was Normandy that rekindled my love of plainly boiled potatoes swimming in salty butter, the two ingredients being so tasty. There was a time when the fashion for fancy mash and so forth more or less eclipsed this simplicity, and perhaps boiled potatoes also suffered from the post-war image of meat and two veg, overcooked and bland. So they've taken a little time to reassert themselves as being pretty much the perfect accompaniment to any soupy stew or meaty dish. And be sure to make plenty for the week ahead, as they have endless uses – in a Russian salad (see page 145), a Mussel chowder (see page 56), or Oven-baked, smoked haddock fishcakes (see page 130), for instance.

Buttered potatoes

Serves 6

1.5kg maincrop potatoes, peeled and halved, or
   quartered if large

50g salted butter
sea salt

Bring a large pan of salted water to the boil, add the potatoes and simmer for 20–30 minutes until they are tender.

Drain them into a sieve and leave for a few minutes for the surface moisture to evaporate, then return them to the pan, dot with the butter and leave for a minute or two for it to melt.
If cooking extra potatoes for another recipe, toss with butter only as much potato as you need for the immediate meal.

Gail Mejia, who founded Baker & Spice, spawned a wave of 'boutique' patisseries, serving fabulous breads, hearty cakes and colourful salads. These potatoes are typical of her Lebanese-inspired food, and the best roasties I have tasted in a long while. Perfect for a barbecue, they are as good cold as hot, and at any temperature in between. They are pictured on page 120.

Herb roasties

Serves 6

1.5kg floury maincrop potatoes, peeled
   and halved, or quartered lengthways
sea salt and black pepper

5 tbsp olive oil
1 tbsp each of chopped rosemary and
   thyme leaves

Heat the oven to 240°C (220°C fan oven) gas mark 9. Boil the potatoes for 7 minutes in a pan of well-salted water, drain and leave for a few minutes for the surface moisture to evaporate, then give them a good shake in the pan.

Pour over the olive oil, add the chopped herbs and some salt and pepper and toss to coat them.

Spread out the potatoes, spacing them slightly apart, on a couple of baking trays and roast for 30–40 minutes, turning them every 10 minutes.

There is no accompaniment that suits a slowly roasted joint or casserole quite like a big bowl of cabbage. Of all the varieties, Savoy cabbage has to be the first choice, and I can never resist adding caraway and chilli, which seem to bring out the best in it.

Cabbage with caraway seeds

Serves 4–6

1 Savoy cabbage
½ tsp caraway seeds
2 tbsp extra virgin olive oil, or rendered duck or
 pork fat

a small pinch of dried chilli flakes
sea salt
3 tbsp water

Trim the base and remove the outer leaves from the cabbage, then quarter it, cut out the core and finely slice the leaves (as they are so tightly packed I tend not to bother to wash them).

Give the caraway seeds a light pounding in a pestle and mortar to break them up. Heat the olive oil or fat in a large saucepan over a medium heat, add the caraway and chilli and give it a stir, then add the cabbage, season with salt and stir-fry for a couple of minutes until it is glossy.

Add the water, clamp on a saucepan lid and cook over a low heat for 15 minutes, or until the cabbage is tender, stirring halfway through. The cabbage is quite good-natured and can be reheated if wished. Any leftovers make a delicious bubble and squeak.

I recently came across a recipe for mash with as much butter as potato in it, which I can only imagine tastes sublime. I mention that to justify the quantity of cream here, but it really is worth it. Champ is pictured on page 90.

Champ

Serves 4

900g floury potatoes
3 bunches spring onions, sliced
100g unsalted butter
200ml double cream

sea salt and black pepper

Boil the potatoes until tender, then pass through a mouli. Sweat the spring onions in the butter for 5 minutes. Add the cream and cook for a few minutes longer, then season and stir into the mash.

A few years back I found myself on a farm in Sicily midsummer, when the whole kitchen had been turned into a factory for a couple of days, to produce and bottle tomato sauce. Empty green wine bottles had been saved over the months, and were lined up ready to receive the thin, fresh purée that was one of the standbys of their cooking. Over the next few days it made a discreet appearance in all manner of dishes: young artichokes were stuffed and braised in it, and tiny squid were cooked in a stew of it, while plates of pasta soaked it up before being confettied with crisp breadcrumbs. For this Sicilian kitchen, where there was tomato sauce there was dinner.

It's a sentiment I can relate to – when the last of a batch of fresh tomato sauce has been used up, the options for supper seem that much narrower. My own take on it is similar to a passata, but that much richer. I like to reduce the purée by about half with a generous addition of butter or olive oil, until it is concentrated and intense. As a sauce for pasta, its thin, pale appearance belies its full-on sweetness; for children it's nirvana, while forming the basis for gutsier sauces for the staunch of palate.

During the winter months I usually make this sauce with cherry tomatoes for a treat, but during the summer months we're spoilt for choice. And you needn't give up any real beauties that you have been saving to make into a salad; slightly overripe or, for that matter, underripe fruits are both excellent candidates. Rather than bottle the sauce with all the palaver of sterilising, I prefer to freeze it.

Fresh tomato sauce

Makes approx. 800ml

1.35kg tomatoes, halved
1 tsp caster sugar
1 heaped tsp sea salt

100g unsalted butter plus 4 tbsp olive oil, or
100ml extra virgin olive oil

Place the tomatoes in a medium saucepan, cover and cook over a low heat for 20–30 minutes, stirring them occasionally, until they collapse.

Pass the cooked tomatoes through a sieve or a mouli-légumes and return to the pan, washing it out if necessary.

Add the sugar, salt and butter plus 4 tbsp olive oil, or the 100ml extra virgin olive oil, and then simmer very gently, uncovered, for 60 minutes until thickened but still of a thin, pouring consistency. Use fresh, or leave to cool, then freeze.

Pickles deserve a light hand; it's one thing to preserve a vegetable for months on end, another if it is so aggressive that it dominates whatever it is served with. You can make a pickle to eat straight away, simply by lightly poaching fresh vegetables in a solution of a half or a third vinegar mixed with water and a few aromatics in the way of whole spices, garlic cloves, chillies and woody herbs. Dress them with olive oil once they are cool, and they are ready to accompany a selection of antipasti, cold duck or lamb for lunch the same day. They can also be preserved for a limited time by covering them with olive oil, a small luxury that is delicious to dip into with bread or can be used for a salad dressing. Two treats for the trouble of making one.

Peppers in oil

Makes 2 x 500 ml jars

300ml white wine vinegar or
  cider vinegar
700ml water
1 tsp sea salt
1 head of garlic, cloves peeled

4–5 red or yellow peppers, cored, seeds and
  membranes removed, and cut into long,
  wide strips
a couple of handfuls of basil leaves
180g pitted green olives
about 500ml extra virgin olive oil

Pour the vinegar into a medium saucepan, add the water and salt and bring to the boil. Add the garlic and half the peppers and bring back to the boil, then simmer for 8 minutes. Remove the peppers with a slotted spoon (leaving the garlic in the pan) and drain on a clean tea towel, cupped-side down. Cook the remainder of the peppers in the same fashion, then drain with the garlic.

While the peppers are cooking, heat two 0.5 litre Le Parfait jars (or whatever jars you are using) for 5 minutes in a medium to hot oven at 190°C (170°C fan oven) gas mark 5. Cover the base of the jars with a few of the pepper slices, cupped-side up, a couple of basil leaves, poached garlic cloves and olives. Pour over enough olive oil almost to cover them, then press the peppers down with the back of a spoon. Repeat with the remaining ingredients, pushing the peppers down each time you add the olive oil to submerge them. Finally, cover the vegetables with a few millimetres of olive oil and close the jars.

The pickles can be eaten immediately, or stored in the fridge for up to one month. The oil will harden, but liquefy at room temperature. Once opened, store the jars in the fridge for up to a week, making sure the vegetables are submerged beneath the oil.

A favourite ruse for dealing with a glut of tomatoes is to slow-roast them until they are sublimely sweet and intense. The moment of madness of sun-dried tomatoes is all but over – thankfully you hardly even see them for sale any longer, but the idea of concentrating the flavour of tomatoes in a mock-dried fashion with a long spell in a gentle oven seems a positive legacy. These are one of those glam accessories with endless potential: surround them with goat's cheese, olives, some air-dried ham and a good loaf of bread and it's the difference between a snack and lunch.

Slow-roasted tomatoes

Serves 6

1.5kg medium-sized tomatoes
4 garlic cloves, skin on, crushed
5 sprigs of thyme
sea salt

caster sugar
extra virgin olive oil
a handful of basil leaves

Heat the oven to 140°C (120°C fan oven) gas mark 1. Bring a large pan of water to the boil. Cut out a cone from the top of each tomato to remove the core, plunge them into the boiling water for 20 seconds (you may need to do this in batches) and then into cold water. Drain them and slip off the skins, then halve and deseed them.

Lay out the tomato halves on a non-stick baking tray, scatter over the garlic and thyme and season with salt and a sprinkling of sugar. Then drizzle over 4 tbsp of olive oil and bake them for 1–2 hours, turning the trays around if they seem to be colouring unevenly.

Once they are cool, place them in a bowl or a jar interspersed with the basil leaves, and cover with olive oil. If you are not serving them immediately, cover and chill for up to 3 days, bringing them back up to room temperature before serving.

7
Something Sweet

This trifle fast-tracks to the good bits, the cake and custard, which when they are homemade make an exquisite combination. In tradition it lies somewhere between an Italian and a British trifle. Should you chance across soft Amaretti biscuits, these are the perfect consistency for this recipe, and a first choice. Other than that it relies on a thick, unctuous custard. And the only secret here is to thicken it without boiling, which would render the custard gloopy and overly thick, rather than silky.

Italian trifle

Serves 6

For the custard
6 large egg yolks
125g icing sugar, sifted
75g plain flour, sifted
650ml full-cream milk
3 strips of lemon peel
1½ tsp vanilla extract
4 tbsp dark rum

For the sponge cake
50g plain flour
a pinch of sea salt
3 large eggs
75g golden caster sugar

To assemble
25g golden caster sugar
100g Amaretti biscuits,
    preferably soft
100g good raspberry jam
150ml whipping cream
1 tbsp flaked almonds,
    toasted

To make the custard, whisk the egg yolks and icing sugar together in a medium, non-stick saucepan until smooth, then whisk in the flour a third at a time, until you have a thick, creamy paste.

Bring the milk to the boil in a small saucepan with the lemon peel and whisk it into the egg mixture a little at a time until it has all been incorporated. Cook for a few minutes on a low heat until the custard thickens, stirring vigorously with a wooden spoon. If necessary, you can give it a quick whisk. The custard shouldn't actually boil, but the odd bubble will ensure that it's hot enough to thicken properly. Cook it for a few minutes longer, stirring constantly.

Off the heat, stir in the vanilla and 2 tablespoons of the rum. Discard the lemon zest, pour the custard into a bowl, cover and leave to cool.

To make the sponge, heat the oven to 200°C (180°C fan oven) gas mark 6. Butter a 23cm sandwich tin with a removable base. Sift the flour into a bowl with the salt. Place the eggs and caster sugar in a bowl and whisk for about 8 minutes, using an electric whisk, until the mixture is almost white and mousse-like. Lightly fold in the flour in two goes.

Transfer the mixture to the prepared tin, and give it a couple of sharp taps to eliminate any large bubbles. Bake for 12–14 minutes until lightly golden, springy to the touch and shrinking from the sides. Run a knife around the collar to loosen it, then leave to cool.

To assemble the trifle, pour 25ml boiling water over the caster sugar and stir to dissolve, then stir in the remaining rum. Break the Amaretti into a bowl and sprinkle over half the rum syrup. Spread a couple of tablespoons of custard over the base of a 20cm trifle bowl. Break up half the cake and arrange on the base of the bowl, so it is partially covered. Sprinkle over half the remaining rum syrup, spread with half the jam and scatter over half the Amaretti. Spread with half the custard and repeat with the remaining half of the ingredients. Whisk the cream until it is stiff, then smooth it over the top. Cover and chill overnight. Just before serving, sprinkle over the almonds.

Lying halfway between a tiramisú and a trifle, this makes a great party piece, and can be made the day beforehand. I would choose to serve it with a bowl of raspberries or blackberries, both of which complement chocolate beautifully. Or maybe you have a handful of wild strawberries in your border to call on.

However tasty chocolate with a high-percentage of cocoa may be, it will wreak havoc when you introduce other ingredients to the melted chocolate – for instance, when making a mousse. I know this from bitter experience, having ended up with one too many indecorous claggy lumps. Though it is logical if you consider that dry cocoa solids behave in the same way as flour. So it is worth playing it safe by using chocolate with a lower percentage of cocoa – check the small print on the wrapper.

Dark chocolate trifle

Serves 6

200g dark chocolate, about 50% cocoa,
   broken into pieces
5 medium eggs, separated
250ml strong fresh black coffee, cooled
125ml Kahlua or Tia Maria

125ml single cream
1 x 200g packet sponge fingers
   (boudoir biscuits)
70g white chocolate, coarsely grated
raspberries, to serve

Place the chocolate in a large bowl set over a pan of simmering water and heat gently until it melts. Remove from the heat and whisk in the egg yolks. Combine the cold coffee and Kahlua or Tia Maria in a shallow bowl. Stir a tablespoon of this into the chocolate mixture, and then stir in the single cream. Whisk the egg whites in another large bowl until they are stiff (I use a hand-held electric whisk for this), then fold them a third at a time into the chocolate mixture.

Smear a spoon or two of the chocolate mousse over the base of a 1.5 litre shallow dish (such as a 30cm oval gratin dish). Dip the sponge fingers, a few at a time, into the coffee-liqueur mixture to soak them, and cover the base of the dish, using up half of them. Pour over half the chocolate mousse, then repeat with the remaining sponge fingers and mousse so there are two layers of each. You will probably use up all the liquor – should you run out, make up a little more. Scatter over the white chocolate.

Cover the trifle and chill for at least two hours, or overnight. Serve scattered with raspberries.

A lovely pud come Christmas. If children are going to eat it, you can always leave out the liqueur from the creams, and splash it over at the end for adults. In the interests of snowy whiteness you want a refined white sugar here, and by contrast, the redder the pomegranate, the better – the colour of the outside is usually a good indicator of what lies within.

Panna cotta with orange

Serves 6

600g crème fraîche
2 x 5cm strips of orange zest
90g caster sugar
½ of a sachet of gelatine (or sufficient leaves to
    set 300ml liquid*)

8 tbsp Cointreau or Grand Marnier
1 pomegranate, halved

Bring the crème fraîche, orange zest and sugar to the boil in a small saucepan, stirring occasionally as the cream melts and the sugar dissolves. Leave to stand for 10 minutes, then discard the zest.

Sprinkle the gelatine over a couple of tablespoons of boiling water in a small bowl and leave to dissolve for a few minutes. If it hasn't dissolved completely, stand the bowl inside a second bowl of boiling water and leave it for a few minutes longer, then stir again. Add this to the cream, then mix in 2 tbsp of the liqueur. Divide the cream between six 150ml (9cm) ramekins or little bowls. Cover and leave to cool – I put them into a roasting tray first – then chill overnight or until they set.

To serve, extract the pomegranate seeds by pressing down on the skin and popping them out, removing any pith. Briefly dip the ramekins or bowls into hot water, then run a knife around the edge and turn the creams out onto plates. Splash another tablespoon of Cointreau or Grand Marnier over each panna cotta and scatter with pomegranate seeds.

*If using gelatine leaves, cut them into broad strips, place in a medium-sized bowl, cover with cold water and leave to soak for 5 minutes, then drain. Pour the warm cream over the leaves and stir until they dissolve, then continue as above.

This is a variation on the theme of a crème brûlée, a suave take on custard with apples. I usually settle for the baked custard with some fruit below in lieu of the caramel lid, to avoid having to play with a blowtorch. Some lacy biscuits would go down nicely on the side.

Baked apple and custard pots

Serves 6

650g Bramley apples, peeled,
    cored and sliced
150g golden caster sugar
2 tbsp Calvados or brandy

5 medium egg yolks
500ml single cream
2 cloves, ground to a powder

Place the apples with 100g of the sugar in a medium saucepan. Cover and cook over a low heat for 15–20 minutes until they're soft, then mash them up with a spoon. If there is any residual liquid, simmer uncovered until the purée dries out, stirring frequently towards the end to make sure it doesn't catch. Stir in the Calvados or brandy and leave to cool, then divide the apple between six 150ml (9cm) ramekins.

    Heat the oven to 160°C (140°C fan oven) gas mark 3. Whisk the egg yolks and remaining sugar together in a medium-sized bowl. Heat the cream in a small saucepan almost to boiling point, then whisk it into the egg and sugar mixture, which will instantly thicken a little. Strain it into a jug and stir in the ground cloves. (Whole cloves freshly ground in a pestle and mortar will be that much more pungent than ready-ground ones.)

    Gently pour the custard on top of the apple over the back of a spoon, so as not to disturb it. Place the ramekins in a roasting dish with warm water to come two-thirds of the way up the sides, and bake for 1 hour until set and lightly golden on the surface. The pots can be served at room temperature, or chilled, in which case they can be made a day or two in advance.

Like the best fruit pies, this is short and crumbly on top, full of meltingly tender fruit below, giving way to slightly soggy pastry seeped in juices underneath. Depending on how confident you are with pastry, the butter can be stepped up to 250g, which will make it shorter and more delicate to eat, but softer to work with, and a little messier to look at.

Fig and pear pie with vanilla custard

Serves 6

For the sweet shortcrust pastry
150g unsalted butter, softened
150g golden caster sugar
2 medium eggs
400g plain flour, sifted, plus 2 tbsp,
    plus extra for dusting
50g ground almonds
milk for brushing
caster sugar for dusting

For the filling
600g firm but ripe pears, peeled,
    cored and sliced
300g figs, stalks trimmed, quartered
100g light muscovado sugar
juice of ½ lemon

For the vanilla custard
300ml full-cream milk
6 medium egg yolks
75g golden caster sugar
1 vanilla pod
150ml whipping cream

First make the vanilla custard. Pour the milk into a small saucepan and bring to the boil. Whisk the egg yolks and sugar in a bowl, then whisk in the milk. Return this to the pan and heat gently until you have a thin pouring custard that coats the back of a spoon, taking care not to overheat it. Pour it into a bowl straight away. Slit the vanilla pod, cut it up and add to the custard, then cover with clingfilm and leave to cool. Liquidise and sieve the custard. Whip the cream and whisk it in, then cover and chill until needed.

Using a wooden spoon, cream the butter and sugar for the pastry together in a bowl until soft and fluffy. Alternatively, a food processor or mixer will make light work of this. Beat in the eggs until well combined, then gradually add the 400g of flour and the ground almonds and bring the dough together. Wrap it in clingfilm and chill for at least 2 hours – it will keep for several days.

When ready to cook, heat the oven to 190°C (170°C fan oven) gas mark 5. Allow the dough to come to room temperature and then knead it until pliable on a lightly floured surface. Thinly roll out two-thirds of the dough and use this to line the base of a shallow 30cm oval (1.6 litre) gratin dish, letting the extra hang over the sides. You can, if you like, trim off the excess at this point. Don't worry if the dough tears and you end up partly pressing it into the dish.

Sprinkle the 2 tablespoons of flour over the pears in a bowl and toss, then mix in the figs, brown sugar and lemon juice. Tip the fruit into the pie dish and arrange it evenly over the base. Roll out the remaining third of pastry with the trimmings and lay it over the top. I find it easiest to wrap it around the rolling pin and lift it up. Press the pastry together at the rim, and trim it leaving 1cm for shrinkage, then crimp the edge using the tips of your fingers or the tip of a knife.

Roll out some trimmings to cut out fig shapes and leaves. Brush the undersides with milk and secure them to the pie. Dust with caster sugar and bake the pie for 40–50 minutes until golden.

Stir the custard before serving with the pie.

Primroses, little chicks and yellow satin ribbons are the stuff the Easter table is made of, and in keeping with that so is a syrupy sponge wafting the scent of saffron. You can make this a day or two ahead and steam it for half an hour to reheat, or even freeze it. In this case, remove the paper once it is cooked, cover it with clingfilm and put fresh paper on to rewarm. Otherwise I would be inclined to cook it before lunch or dinner and leave it standing in the pan. Custard devotees should turn to page 186.

Steamed saffron syrup sponge

Serves 6

a good pinch of saffron filaments (about 30)
100ml full-cream milk
120g unsalted butter, diced
100g golden caster sugar
1 medium egg

180g plain flour
1 heaped tsp baking powder
50g sultanas
2 tbsp golden syrup
crème fraîche or clotted cream, to serve

Grind the saffron filaments in a pestle and mortar. Bring the milk to the boil in a small saucepan, pour it over the saffron and leave to infuse for 15 minutes.

Meanwhile, cream the butter and sugar together in a food processor, then incorporate the egg. Sift in the flour and baking powder, then add the saffron infusion. Transfer the mixture to a bowl and stir in the sultanas.

Butter a 1.2 litre pudding basin and line the bottom with a square of baking paper. Spoon the syrup into the base and place the pudding mixture on top, smoothing the surface. Cut out a circle of baking paper to cover the surface of the pudding, with several inches to spare on either side. Butter the centre of one side, lay it buttered-side down on top of the pudding bowl, and tightly tie the paper in place with string just below the rim. (A helping hand is always welcome with this bit.) Place in a large saucepan with boiling water to come two-thirds of the way up the sides of the pudding, cover and simmer over a low heat for 1½ hours.

To unmould the pudding, remove the paper and run a knife around the edge, then invert it onto a plate and remove the square of paper on the bottom. Serve with crème fraîche or clotted cream.

Fruitcakes hold a fascination for me, in part because they belong to that sophisticated world of British dishes beloved of Continentals, who have impeccable taste in recognising world classics when they encounter them. Italians rave over our summer pudding, and cannot get enough Stilton, and I now give Christmas puddings or cakes to all my French neighbours, as there is no equivalent there. Fruitcakes are strange creations, and it's hard to believe that the sloppy, boiled mixture that goes into the tin can possibly emerge from the oven as the masterpiece it does a few hours later.

I believe this particular recipe is all the better for the absence of eggs and refined sugar, all its sweetness being drawn from the dates and dried fruits that also account for its louche density. As with mincemeat, you can tinker with the original to suit your own taste. Dried cranberries and sour cherries, as well as being deliciously lively little fruits, bring it into the modern world, and you may have access to some classy glacé fruits, or like to add some nuts.

Anything that matures also fascinates by carrying with it an air of connoisseurship. A fruitcake can be made several months in advance, and fed with teasing quantities of brandy or other eau-de-vie as time goes on. The idea here is to infuse it with ever more booze, so it becomes richer and stronger by the week. It's a treat of a ritual, peeling back the layers of crinkly baking paper and drawing in its heady scent. Although this aspect does, I think, sometimes put off the would-be cook, who feels compelled to make it months in advance, when in truth fruitcakes are equally delicious eaten as soon as they are made – just that much fresher in flavour and crumbly, which is no bad thing.

The kind of fruitcake that goes down best in our house is indecently moist and sticky. This example stands on its own without any marzipan and icing, and offers the same level of indulgence as a chocolate cake (though, as you will see in the recipe for Chocolate fruit charlotte on page 195, you can combine the two).

Sticky fruitcake

Makes 1 x 20cm cake

300g unsalted butter, plus extra for greasing
500ml apple juice
300g pitted and chopped dates
350g raisins
325g sultanas
1 tsp bicarbonate of soda

150g plain flour, sifted
150g ground almonds
½ tsp freshly grated nutmeg
finely grated zest of 1 orange and 1 lemon
icing sugar for dusting (optional)

Preheat the oven to 160°C (140°C fan oven) gas mark 3, and butter a 20cm cake tin 9cm deep, with a removable base. Line the base with baking paper and butter this also.

Melt the butter in a medium saucepan with the apple juice, then stir in the dates, raisins and sultanas. Bring to the boil, then simmer over a low heat for 5 minutes. Transfer the mixture to a large mixing bowl and stir in the bicarbonate of soda – it will fizz furiously. Leave it to cool for 10 minutes.

Beat the flour, ground almonds and nutmeg into the dried fruit mixture. Fold in the citrus zest and transfer the mixture to the prepared cake tin, smoothing the surface.

Tear off a sheet of baking paper large enough to cover the surface of the cake and go about halfway down the sides of the tin. Cut out a small circle from the centre about 2cm in diameter, then butter the surface that will come in contact with the cake as it rises. Lay it over the top of the tin and tie it in place with string.

Bake the cake for 2 hours, until a skewer inserted into the centre comes out clean. Run a knife around the collar, remove it and leave the cake to cool on the base. It will be good to eat from the following day onwards. If you're not planning to cover it with marzipan and icing, then you may like to give it a quick shower of icing sugar shortly before serving. It will keep well in a tin or covered container for several weeks.

Hard to believe that fruitcake could get any stickier, but here's how. For a dramatic spectacle you could also flame the honey-fried fruitcake with a little brandy or eau-de-vie. Heat the spirit in a ladle over a gas hob until it ignites and then pour it, little by little, over the cake.

Honey-fried fruitcake with ice cream

Serves 4

a knob of unsalted butter
1 tbsp runny honey

4 slices fruitcake (see Sticky fruitcake, page 191)
vanilla ice cream, to serve

Heat the butter with the honey in a frying pan over a medium heat and fry the fruitcake slices for a minute or two on either side, turning them carefully with a spatula, until surrounded by a glossy caramel.

Serve the syrupy pan juices spooned over the cake, with a scoop of ice cream on top.

This streusel of juicy black cherries nestling between layers of meltingly short crumble is a treat. For the full treatment, try it newly cooled with a spoonful of clotted cream. It's a good dish for a picnic, in which case you can transport the cake in its tin.

Cherry streusel

Serves 6–8

200g self-raising flour
110g ground almonds
110g golden caster sugar
½ tsp ground cinnamon

225g unsalted butter, chilled and diced
400g cherries, pitted
icing sugar for dusting

Heat the oven to 190°C (170°C fan oven) gas mark 5. Place the flour, ground almonds, caster sugar and cinnamon in the bowl of a food processor. Add the butter and reduce the mixture to crumbs (it's very important that the butter is cold, otherwise it will cream into a dough), stopping the motor as they start to cling together like a crumble. You can also prepare the mixture by hand.

Press half the mixture into the base of a 20cm cake tin, 9cm deep, with a removable base. Scatter the cherries over the shortbread base, then scatter the remaining crumble mixture over the top of the fruit and bake for 45 minutes until the top is golden and crisp.

Remove and allow the cake to cool in the tin, then run a knife around the collar to remove it, dust with icing sugar and serve.

I feel like a child returning to her first-ever recipe when I cook this chocolate cake from Simone Beck and Julia Child's *Mastering the Art of French Cooking* Volume Two. It's a cake within a cake, which takes as its starting point leftover or slightly stale fruitcake. I like to serve it for pudding with chocolate sauce or cream.

Chocolate fruit charlotte

Makes 1 x 20cm cake

butter for greasing
225g dark chocolate, about 70% cocoa,
   broken into pieces
150ml full-cream milk
225g fruitcake, crumbled
2 tbsp dark rum
4 medium eggs, separated
¼ tsp cream of tartar
100g golden caster sugar

For the chocolate sauce
180g dark chocolate, about 70% cocoa,
   broken into pieces
150ml whipping cream
6 tbsp strong black coffee

Preheat the oven to 190°C (170°C fan oven) gas mark 5. Butter a 20cm cake tin, 9cm deep, and line the base with baking paper.

Gently melt the chocolate with the milk in a saucepan, whisking until smooth, then stir in the cake and rum and transfer to a bowl.

Using an electric whisk, whisk the egg whites in a bowl until they start to rise, then add the cream of tartar and continue to whisk until firm. Sprinkle over 3 tablespoons of the sugar, one at a time, whisking well with each addition until you have a glossy meringue.

In another bowl, whisk the yolks and remaining sugar until pale and thick.

Beat the egg yolk mixture into the chocolate mixture. Now fold in about a quarter of the meringue to loosen the cake mixture, then fold in the remainder.

Transfer the mixture to the prepared tin and bake for 50–60 minutes until a skewer inserted into the centre comes out with just a few moist crumbs clinging to it.

Run a knife around the collar, leave to cool for 20 minutes, then remove the cake. It will keep for several days in an airtight container.

To make the sauce, gently melt the chocolate in a bowl set over a saucepan of simmering water. Add the cream and coffee and continue to heat together, whisking until you have a smooth sauce. The sauce can be made in advance and reheated, in which case cover and chill it once cold. Serve the cake warm, about an hour out of the oven, or at room temperature, with the sauce.

There is little doubt that the more you do something, the easier it becomes. And overcoming my fear of making pancakes had everything to do with motherhood. I went from making them on an occasional basis, haphazardly, trusting in the first recipe that came to hand, to being able to whisk up a batter and churn out a batch at the whim and demand of my five-year-old. For children, pancakes are one of life's great joys, not just for enjoying on on Shrove Tuesday. They can be guaranteed to raise a sunny smile on the rainiest of days, at breakfast, lunch, or tea. And while five-year-olds may get the first call, there are invariably plenty of adults waiting in the wings to gratefully receive any that haven't been claimed.

The accessibility of pancakes is writ large in their ingredients, which we all, except in moments of extreme dearth, have to hand. Eggs, milk, flour and butter is the roll-call fundamental to British batters, the starting point for not only pancakes but Yorkshire puds and toad-in-the-hole. And, as with any profoundly simple food, the quality of the ingredients is everything. It's a good opportunity for a fine butter and a rich milk with a good head of cream on it. I would hesitate to strive for ultra-thin pancakes, achieved in part by cutting the milk with water, as the results are of negligible improvement in delicacy, and because of the heartache of cooking anything that flimsy, I would say not worth it. A perfectly delicate pancake can be achieved with milk as the sole liquid.

Foolproof classic pancakes

Makes about 16

250g plain flour
1 tbsp golden caster sugar
a pinch of sea salt

3 large eggs and 2 egg yolks
600ml full-cream milk
40g unsalted butter, melted

To prepare the pancakes by hand, place the flour, sugar and salt in a large bowl, add the eggs and yolks and mix to a lumpy wet paste using a spoon. Now whisk in the milk, a little to begin with to smooth out the lumps, then in bolder streams once you have a creamy batter. Alternatively, place all the ingredients except the butter in a blender and whizz until smooth. Give the sides and bottom of the blender a stir to make sure no flour is clinging, and whizz again. Transfer the batter to a bowl if you've made it in a blender. Leave the batter to stand for at least 30 minutes, then stir in the melted butter.

Heat a frying pan with an 18cm base (a 24cm pan) over a medium-high heat for several minutes, and if you want to speed things up, have two on the go.

Ladle in just enough batter to coat the base, tipping it to allow it to run evenly over the surface. When the pan is hot enough, the pancake mixture should sizzle as it hits the pan. Cook for 30 seconds until the top side appears dry and lacy at the edges and it is golden and lacy underneath. Loosen the edges using a palette knife or spatula, then slip this underneath and flip the pancake over. Give it another 30 seconds and then slip it onto a plate. I always discard the first one – for no explicable reason it never seems to work properly – and it's only once you've done three or four that you really get into the swing of it. Cook the remainder likewise.

You can either dish up the pancakes as they are cooked, or pile them up on a plate and cover with foil to keep warm. I quite often make them in advance, cover and chill them once they are cool, and reheat them briefly on each side in a dry frying pan. In this case they keep well for several days.

Whether you serve them rolled or folded is largely a cultural consideration. I come down in favour of the latter, in French tradition, cradled in a napkin to avoid burnt fingers.

Sweet ideas

At their simplest, dab them with unsalted butter
Sprinkle with golden caster sugar and squeeze over a little lemon
Drizzle with maple or golden syrup
Spread with raspberry or apricot jam
Sprinkle over grated dark chocolate
As a short cut for kids, sprinkle with a little drinking chocolate powder

This is a real extravaganza: use it as a showpiece as the finale to a special dinner, or presented with candles as a birthday cake. It's a stack of pancakes spread with chocolate sauce in between each one and smothered with more sauce as the stack comes out of the oven. Cut through, it reveals an exquisite millefeuille of layers.

Chocolate pancake millefeuille

Serves 8

16 pancakes (see Foolproof classic pancakes, page 197), cooked and cooled

For the chocolate sauce
250g dark chocolate, 50% cocoa, broken up

50g unsalted butter, diced
170ml full-cream milk
50ml double cream
100ml strong black coffee
50g caster sugar

To make the chocolate sauce, place the chocolate in a bowl set over a pan of simmering water and gently melt it. Whisk in the butter, and once this has melted whisk in the milk, cream, coffee and sugar. Transfer the sauce to a bowl, cover the surface with clingfilm and set aside until required. It will firm up to the consistency of double cream as it cools.

To assemble the pudding, spread a little chocolate sauce on the base of a gratin dish, as wide as the pancakes, then layer the pancakes, spreading each one with about 1½ tablespoons of the chocolate sauce. Expect this to ooze out into the bottom of the dish as the stack gets higher. You should have about a third of the sauce left over at the end. Cover the pancake stack with foil. You can prepare the pudding to this point several hours in advance, in which case set it aside somewhere cool.

To serve it, heat the oven to 170°C (150°C fan oven) gas mark 3, and reheat the pudding for 20–25 minutes.

In the meantime, gently reheat the remaining chocolate sauce in a small saucepan.

Remove the foil and coat the surface of the pancake stack with the sauce, allowing it to run down the sides. Serve straight away, cut into wedges like a cake.

These pudgy, slightly sour pancakes are blini-like in their charm. I like to slather them in salty butter and honeycomb. But on another occasion, they are also good as an appetiser with smoked fish or roe.

Buckwheat pancakes with salted butter and honey

Serves 8 (makes 25)

80g plain flour
80g buckwheat flour
   (see Suppliers, page 204)
a pinch of sea salt
a pinch of golden caster sugar
2 tsp baking powder
I medium egg, separated

300ml full-cream milk
groundnut oil

To serve
softened, salted butter
honeycomb

Sift the dry ingredients into a large bowl. Whisk the egg yolk and milk in another bowl until blended. Pour this mixture onto the sifted dry ingredients and whisk until smooth. Leave to stand for 10 minutes, then whisk the egg white until it holds soft peaks and fold it into the pancake mixture.

In the meantime, heat a cast-iron frying pan or flat griddle on a lowish heat for 10 minutes until it reaches an even, snug warmth. Grease the hot iron with groundnut oil, then drop tablespoons of the mixture into the pan, spaced slightly apart. Cook for 1–2 minutes until the surface pits with bubbles, then carefully turn the pancakes using a palette knife and cook for about 1 minute more until golden on the underside. You should find that the first side is completely smooth, while the underside looks more like a crumpet.

Remove them to a plate, smear with a little salted butter and a dollop of honeycomb, and eat while you put some more on to cook, re-oiling the pan now and again between batches as it needs it. Or, if you are making them in advance, keep them covered with foil on a plate for up to half an hour. They can also be reheated in an oven warmed to 160°C (140°C fan oven) gas mark 3. Stack them about six high, wrap in foil and heat for 20 minutes.

Suppliers

Fish

Fresh fish direct

If you are in doubt about the source of your fish, or if you have difficulty obtaining it, **Cornish Fish Direct** supply fish harvested by environmentally friendly methods, and some boats fish directly for them. Methods include hand-line, long-line, crab potting, and fishing for selective species, such as pilchard drift-netting and day-boat trawling. The fish are filleted to order and delivered within 24 hours of being caught. Cornish Fish Direct can supply both Cornish sardines and pilchards.
- For mail order tel: 01736 332112
- Email: enquiries@pilchardworks.co.uk
- www.pilchardworks.co.uk

Organic trout

Hawkshead Trout Farm in the Lake District were the first to rear rainbow trout organically. Their flesh is that much firmer thanks to being reared in plentiful space, which lowers their stress levels and in turn reduces the incidence of disease. And, like organic salmon, they are pale in colour, almost white, without resort to artificial colours. Available by mail order from **Graig Farm Organics**.
- For mail order tel: 01597 851655
- www.graigfarm.co.uk

Smoked salmon

Fergus and Anne Granville run their **Hebridean Smokehouse** on North Uist, smoking carefully reared salmon and sea trout over peat cut from the Uist moors, where it has formed over millennia. Since the Outer Hebrides are virtually treeless, peat is the traditional fuel. This very British cure is feisty, and only small fish are selected – a different tale to the bland, pink smoked salmon of Norway.
Hebridean Smokehouse Ltd, Clachan, Locheport, Isle of North Uist, HS6 5DH.
- For mail order tel: 01876 580209
- email: sales@hebrideansmokehouse.com
- www.hebrideansmokehouse.com

Cheese

Cheese direct

Paxton & Whitfield can be relied upon to have matured their cheeses to perfection. You can visit one of their shops in Jermyn Street, London; John Street, Bath; Wood Street, Stratford-upon-Avon, or The Mailbox, Birmingham.
- For mail order tel: 0870 264 2101
- www.paxtonandwhitfield.co.uk

Goat's cheese

Neal's Yard Dairy sell a stunning range of British goat's cheeses, including Woolsery and Ticklemore, lovely buttery hard goat's cheeses that hold their own when melted, and Ragstone, a softer goat's cheese more like a Crottin, which melts to a creamy river.
- For mail order tel: 0207 500 7653
- Email: mailorder@nealsyarddairy.co.uk
- www.nealsyarddairy.co.uk

Meat and poultry

Late-season lamb

Askerton Castle Estate,
Brampton, Cumbria CA8 2BD.

- For mail order tel: 016977 3332
- www.askertoncastle.co.uk

Whitby Steads Hill Farm,
Askham, Penrith, Cumbria CA10 2PG.
- For mail order tel: 01931 712051
- www.whitbysteads.co.uk

North Highland Fine Lamb.
- For mail order tel: 01863 766505
- www.finelamb.co.uk

Salt-marsh lamb

Salt-marsh-grazed lamb, known in its controlled area of France as pré-salé, is only just beginning to get the recognition it deserves here. Its flesh is lean and dense, rendered particularly juicy by the salt on the sea-washed grasses on which the lambs feed. They are herded off it at high tide, which also means that they get more exercise than other sheep. Lambs sold by the half or whole are available mail order from:

The **Holker Estate**, where they graze around the coast of the Cartmel Peninsula.
- For mail order tel: 015395 58313
- www.holker-hall.co.uk

Draenogan Mawr through **Snowdonia Mountain Lamb**, where they graze on the estuary opposite Port Meirion.
- For mail order tel: 01341 241469
- Email: mail@snowdonialamb.f9.co.uk
- www.snowdonialamb.f9.co.uk

Meat direct

The Scottish retailer **Donald Russell** has been providing us with superlative beef and lamb for years. His company also sells old-fashioned, slow-cooking cuts such as oxtail, brisket and tongue.

Donald Russell, Harlaw Road, Inverurie, Aberdeenshire AB51 4FR.
- For mail order tel: 01467 629666
- Email: order@donaldrusselldirect.com
- www.donaldrussell.co.uk

Buccleuch Estates also supply Scottish beef by mail order.
- For mail order tel: 01556 502 555
- www.buccleuchfoods.com

Air-dried ham

As the curers of Duchy Originals bacon, **Denhay Farms'** reputation precedes it. But their air-dried ham came first in 1987. Similar to Italian and Spanish hams, it has a lovely sweet aromatic savour of its own. They cure outdoor-reared British pigs in Bramley apple juice, local honey and herbs, before smoking them over beechwood chips.

Denhay Farms Ltd, Broadoak, Bridport, Dorset DT6 5NP.
- For mail order tel: 01308 458963
- Email: sales@denhay.co.uk
- www.denhay.co.uk

Hams

There is a great deal of controversy over the inclusion of nitrates and nitrites in food, potassium nitrate or saltpetre being the best-known compound – more engagingly, a constituent of gunpowder. In hams, through a complex chemical reaction, nitrites are responsible for the pleasing pink that we associate with this meat. Though some consolation is to be had from the fact that we only use a fraction of the chemical compared to the days of old, potassium nitrate has also been employed as a preservative since the sixteenth century, a role that has diminished with refrigeration. For those who prefer to avoid it, **Swaddles Green Farm** are one of the few companies in the UK to eschew it. Their mild, organically cured hams are prepared using an old-fashioned sweet brine and various aromatics.

- For mail order tel: 0845 456 1768
- Email: info@swaddles.co.uk
- www.swaddles.co.uk

Sausages

You can browse about forty different sausages at any one time at **Crombie's of Edinburgh**'s website. My own hit list begins with Mrs Beaton's Oxford Sausage, a really peppery old-fashioned banger containing veal, lemon and sage, while Auld Reekie has the smokey hit of a frankfurter with the juiciness of a classic breakfast sausage. Their garlicky Toulouse means we never have to cross the Channel again, while the Whisky, Hog and Wild Thyme is every bit as good as it sounds. They can also supply black pudding.
Crombie's of Edinburgh, 97–101 Broughton Street, Edinburgh, Scotland.

- For mail order tel: 0131 557 0111
- www.sausages.co.uk

Sharpham Park include spelt, an ancient form of wheat, in their sausages, made with their organically reared rare breed meat. The sausages are free from artificial preservatives and colouring.

- For mail order tel: 01458 844 080
- Email: info@sharphampark.com
- www.sharphampark.com

Organic chickens

Sheepdrove's Hubbard chickens, a traditional outdoor breed, have a superb flavour and that toothsome quality that is so desirable. The nurseries incorporate conservatories, to acclimatise the young chicks to the big outdoors, where shelter belts cater to their jungle instincts and wariness of open spaces. They are humanely dispatched at 72 days in a water bath run through with an electric current. The chickens come with their giblets on request, and you can also order carcasses for making stock.
Sheepdrove Organic Farm, Lambourn, Berkshire RG17 7UU.

- For mail order tel: 01488 674747
- www.sheepdrove.com

Chutney, honey, mustard

Buccleuch Heritage Foods are to Scotland what Duchy Originals are to England. Made by family and small businesses in and around the Scottish estates of the Duke of Buccleuch, the range plays on traditional flavours and ingredients – poacher's pickle, heather honey and a Scottish crunchy mustard, a loose blend of whole yellow and black seeds.

- For mail order tel: 01556 502 555
- www.buccleuchfoods.com

Curry

Soups such as the mussel pot, which are 'curried' the lazy way with a teaspoon of curry powder, demand the best without having to grind the powder yourself. **Seasoned Pioneers** prepare their blends from around the world.

- For mail order tel: 0800 0682348
- www.seasonedpioneers.co.uk

Buckwheat flour

Buckwheat (*fagopyrum esculentum*) is no relation to wheat and is gluten-free. It is actually a member of the rhubarb family and looks like coarse brown risotto rice.
Doves Farm buckwheat flour is available from major supermarkets.

Index

for salad of grilled
broccoli, dates and
almonds 148–9
for skate and potato
salad tartare 125
drunken guinea fowl
114–15
duck: roast duck with
sauté potatoes 116–17
dumplings
mustard 62–3
sage 52–3

E
eggs *see* custard; frittata;
pancakes; roulade;
soufflé
escabèche, mackerel
122–3

F
fennel: lentil, fennel and
watercress soup 46–7
fig and pear pie with
vanilla custard 186–7
fish
fish pie with capers
140–1
fishcakes: oven-baked
smoked haddock
130–1
jellied fish terrine 19
*see also specific types,
e.g.* skate
foolproof classic
pancakes 196–7
French beans
chicken in a pot 104–5
jellied fish terrine
18–19
tagliardi with pesto,
potatoes and green
beans 34–5
see also salads;
vegetables
fresh tomato sauce
170–1
frittata, courgette 20–1
fruit, dried
steamed saffron syrup
sponge 188–9
sticky fruitcake 190–1
fruitcake
sticky 190–1
honey-fried, with ice
cream 192

G
gammon *see* ham
garlic: Alex Beard's five-
hour roast lamb 68–9
goat's cheese
grilled goat's cheese
and prosciutto rolls
with honey 12–13
roasted beetroot with

toasted goat's
cheese 160–1
twice-baked goat's
cheese and thyme
soufflé 24–5
gratin
cauliflower and
broccoli 164–5
pasta with wild
mushrooms and
bacon 33
gravy, rich brown 65
green beans *see* French
beans
grilled goat's cheese and
prosciutto rolls with
honey 12–13
guinea fowl, drunken
114–15

H
haddock
fish pie with capers
140–1
oven-baked smoked
haddock fishcakes
130–1
ham
air-dried ham and
salad of roasted
roots with caper
dressing 158–9
baked in a crust 78–9
braised ham with a
fondue sauce and
roast onions 76–7
chicken and
mushroom pie
110–13
chicken in a pot
104–5
see also bresaola;
prosciutto
herb roasties 167
honey-fried fruitcake
with ice cream 192

I
ice cream: honey-fried
fruitcake with ice
cream 192
Irish stew 70–1
Italian trifle 178–9

J
jellied fish terrine 18–19

K
kippers, potted 14–15
koftas, lamb 60–1

L
lamb
Alex Beard's five-hour
roast lamb 68–9

casserole of lamb
shanks with
dumplings 62–3
Irish stew 70–1
koftas 60–1
roast leg of lamb with
black olives 66–7
roast loin of lamb
with apricot and
pistachio stuffing
64–5
langoustine stew 134–5
lasagne al forno 82–3
leeks
lettuce and parsley
vichyssoise 40–1
see also vegetables
lentil, fennel and
watercress soup 46–7
lettuce and parsley
vichyssoise 40–1
liver
chicken liver and
apple parfait 16–17
chicken liver pilaf
with pistachios
102–3

M
mackerel escabèche
122–3
marinade
for mackerel
escabèche 122
for prawn brochettes
121
for sticky chicken
wings 97
for vegetable salad
151
marinated vegetable
salad 150–1
Maryland crabcakes
128–9
mayonnaise 127
for Russian salad
144–5
saffron 107
sorrel 139
minestrone 44–5
monkfish: jellied fish
terrine 18–19
mushrooms
braised oxtail and
onions 90–1
and bresaola roulade
22–3
chicken and
mushroom pie
110–13
pasta gratin with wild
mushrooms and
bacon 32–3
pot-roast beef with
mushrooms 86–7

sausage and
mushroom roast
with Stilton-stuffed
potatoes 72–3
mussels
chowder 56–7
curried mussel soup
with saffron 54–5
mustard
dumplings 62–3
sauce 33

N
new potato, roasted red
onion, cashew and
tarragon salad 154–5

O
olives: roast leg of lamb
with black olives 66–7
omelette *see* frittata
onions
braised ham with a
fondue sauce and
roast onions 76–7
braised oxtail and
onions 90–1
new potato, roasted
red onion, cashew
and tarragon salad
155
roasted roots 156–7
roasted squash with
red onion 162–3
salad of grilled
broccoli, dates and
almonds 148–9
spiced slow-roast pork
with orange 74–5
tart 28–9
see also vegetables
oranges
panna cotta with
orange 182–3
spiced slow-roast pork
with orange 74–5
oven-baked, smoked
haddock fishcakes
130–1
oxtail
braised oxtail and
onions 90–1
cottage pie 92–3

P
pak choi: poached
chicken with saffron
mayonnaise 107
pancakes
buckwheat pancakes
with salted butter
and honey 200–1
chocolate pancake
millefeuille 198–9

Picture Credits